THEOLOGIANS TODAY: F. J. SHEED

THEOLOGIANS TODAY: a series selected and edited
by Martin Redfern

F. J. SHEED

SHEED AND WARD · LONDON AND NEW YORK

First published 1972

Sheed & Ward Inc, 64 University Place, New York, N.Y. 10003
and Sheed & Ward Ltd, 33 Maiden Lane, London WC2E 7LA

This selection © Sheed & Ward Ltd, 1972

Nihil obstat: John M. T. Barton, S.T.D., L.S.S
Imprimatur: ✠ Victor Guazzelli, V.G
Westminster, 15 March 1972

Library of Congress Catalog Number 72-2161

This book is set in 12/14 Monotype Imprint

Made and printed in Great Britain by
Billing & Sons Limited, Guildford and London

Contents

Sources and Acknowledgments

"Man and his Context" is from *Theology and Sanity*, London and New York, Sheed & Ward, 1947.

"Born of a Woman" is adapted by the author from *To Know Christ Jesus*, London and New York, Sheed & Ward, 1962, and includes short passages from *God and the Human Condition, I*, and *What Difference does Jesus Make?*

"Scripture in the Church" is from *God and the Human Condition, I: God and the Human Mind*, New York, Sheed & Ward, 1966; and London, Sheed & Ward, 1967.

"Mass and the Eucharist" is from *Is It the Same Church?*, London, Sheed & Ward, 1968; and Dayton, Pflaum, 1968.

INTRODUCTION

The last twenty-five years, and in particular the last ten years, have seen a remarkable flowering of Roman Catholic theology. But for the non-specialist—for the busy parish priest, the active layman, the student—the very wealth of this development presents a range of problems. With which theologian does he begin? Which theologians will he find the most rewarding? Can he ignore any of them?

There are no quick or final answers to such questions, of course, but I hope that this new *Theologians Today* series will help many Catholics to find their own answers more easily. It is designed to achieve two main purposes. Each individual book provides a short but representative introduction to the thought of an outstanding Catholic theologian of the present day, and the series as a whole demonstrates the kind of relationship existing between the best contemporary Catholic theology and official Church teaching.

Both purposes are met by the framework common to all the books. For each book I have selected—and arranged in order of original publication—four pieces which indicate the range in time, approach, and special interest of the theologian concerned. Partly to make my selections more "objective", but mainly to emphasize the close connection between the theologian's writing and the teaching of Vatican ii, I have keyed the articles to the four major documents of that Council—the four Constitutions, on the Church, on Revelation, on the Liturgy, and on the Church in the Modern World.

The selections are very much my own. The theologians themselves, or other editors, would doubtless have made different choices. Nevertheless, I feel that—granted my self-imposed limitations of space and conciliar theme, and the further necessary limitations imposed by copyright or by a proper preference for the out-of-print or inaccessible over the widely available—I have done my own best for men to whom I owe a large debt of gratitude.

F. J. Sheed's originality goes beyond the content of his writing. As author, public speaker, and publisher he has lived out his conviction that theology is not only *for* lay people, but can and should be practised *by* lay people. Readers coming fresh to his writing will quickly notice his stamp in the four articles contained in this volume—his infectious belief that the faith is a faith to be preached with joy, not consigned to textbooks, his deep humanity, his constant desire to help fellow Catholics respond fully and positively to the Church's teaching.

MARTIN REDFERN

8

1. Man and his Context

"Man is not wrong to regard himself as superior to bodily concerns, and as more than a speck of nature or a nameless constituent of the city of man. By his interior qualities he outstrips the whole sum of mere things. . . . God, who probes the heart, awaits him there. There he discerns his proper destiny beneath the eyes of God. When man recognizes in himself a spiritual and immortal soul, he is not being mocked by a deceptive fantasy springing from mere physical or social influences. He is getting to the very truth of the matter."—*Pastoral Constitution on the Church in the Modern World*, I, 1, 14.

Christianity is a historic religion: time has always been its fourth dimension. In studying man's relation with God time is vital. His relation to God has a history, a shape, an unfolding, in fact a plot. It matters enormously when a man was born. It is not a case of a static higher world with which man has had, and could only have, a fixed relation. That world and we have had a good many changes of relation. Things that have happened are part of our religion as well as things that are. Not to know the story is not to know the religion; and not to know the religion is not to know reality. For the facts of religion are not simply facts of religion, but facts, and the most important facts. Given that the context of reality is what it is, it remains for us to study our own being and our own life in it.

I

In summary we can see the context as stateable in terms of three actors and four events. The actors are God, Adam (whether we take him as a man or as Man), Christ: all of them are in us in various ways, and we cannot understand ourselves without understanding them. The events are the Creation, the Fall (whether we take the Genesis story as history encapsulated or as parable), the Redemption, and the Judgment. Knowing this context we know where we are, what we exist for; knowing the totality we can know our place in it and establish our relation to everything else in it. We can do nothing to alter the context, we cannot escape from it. The only thing left to our choice is the mental attitude we shall adopt to it. This is the fundamental choice we have. What choices are open to us? Roughly, three. We can do our best to understand reality, the context in which we are, and harmonize ourselves with it. Or we can understand the context and rebel against it, that is rebel against reality, and what could be bleaker? Or we can ignore the context and either invent one of our own by selecting such elements in the context as we happen, mentally or temperamentally, to find appealing, or else act in no context at all.

Maturity lies with the first choice. Maturity is preparedness to accept reality, co-operate with reality, not kick against reality: remembering that the reality we accept does not mean any situation that merely happens to be, and is in fact within our power to change, but only the vast framework of reality which by God's will is what it is.

We are existent in a universe: we and it alike are

created by God, held in existence from moment to moment by God; we enter life born in Adam and enfolded in the results of his fall: we are meant for a supernatural destiny and can reach it only by entering a supernatural life through rebirth in Christ our Redeemer: we are only ourselves, that is in a condition to be all that we are meant to be and do all that we are meant to do, as members of the Mystical Body of Christ. These are the inescapable facts about ourselves. To be unaware of any element in them is to falsify everything. Whatever one proposes to *do* about the facts, there is only ignorance and error, darkness and double darkness, in not seeing them.

II

In that darkness we cannot get our relation to anything right. The sociologist, for instance, is not *directly* concerned with men's relation to God, but with their relation to one another, and this is true of the novelist, too, for the most part. But men are in fact related to God, fallen in Adam, redeemed by Christ, on their way to Heaven or Hell; and if the novelist or sociologist does not know this, he does not know men, that is he does not know his business. Even what he does see, he does not see right. Our own age is very fastidious about novels, and particularly about their reality. We say a novel is artificial and so saying damn it out of hand, when the characters are unreal. Yet no one seems to mind that the world they inhabit is unreal. The novelist is continually in the absurd position of making laws for his characters in a universe that he did not make, and he is forced to this absurdity simply because he does not know the laws of the real universe. Lacking this knowledge, no matter how profound his insight into human character and passion and motive and motivelessness, he is doomed to unreality. A work of art is not composed in order to illustrate the moral law, any more than a cathedral is built to illustrate mechanical laws. But if the builder ignores the laws of mechanics, his cathedral will show its unreality by falling down; and if the artist ignores the moral law, his work will in the long run show its unreality just as certainly.

This, fundamentally, is why the theologian finds the modern novel chaotic. To one who has grasped the shape of reality, the most solemn, sombre, closely observed modern novel seems as grotesque and fantastic as *Alice in Wonderland*. What makes that masterpiece obviously fantastic is that the law of cause and effect does not operate; but this lack of connection between cause and effect is at the level of the most superficial of secondary causes. Consider what derangement must follow if the first cause is utterly unknown. The grotesqueness is not less because the cause ignored is more fundamental; it is only less obvious because the mind has lost contact with its own depths.

But if the theologian dismisses the novelist's world as lacking shape, the novelist dismisses the theologian's world as lacking flesh and blood. This counter-charge is worth examination, because it draws attention to a real danger that lies in wait for the student of ultimate reality. There *is* a danger that in handling elements so far beyond the reach of daily experience one might come to treat them as abstractions; and in that event our philosophizing would come to be an exercise in getting these abstractions rightly related to one another, in getting the shape of reality right. But the universe is not simply something that has a shape. It is something. The trouble is that the student, in his student days at least, must to a large extent be conditioned by his examinations; and examinations are almost invariably about shape; it is difficult to devise examinations that can test how real reality is to a man. It is possible to have a less detailed knowledge of all the relations that exist between all the various elements of reality, yet know reality better; a man who has never heard of some of the subtler truths may have a far better hold upon reality, because of the intensity of his realization of it. To know all the ins and outs of the diagram of reality is very valuable, but not if reality is in the mind simply as a diagram. We must never mistake intricacy for depth.

Therefore it is necessary to balance our study of the relations of things by a growing intimacy with the very being of things. Thus we must study creation, not simply the process, the transition from nothingness to something by the exercise of God's omnipotence, but the result of the process, the created universe. Studying it, we will come not only to a better knowledge of it, but to a better knowledge of God who created it; and this again not only in the sense already discussed that we learn something of any maker from the thing he has made, but in the less obvious sense that from the study of created being we come to an awareness of *being*, which we can bring to our study of the Uncreated Being. The theologian studying only God might come to a pretty thin notion of God. The primary truth about God is that he is. The more *is* means to us, the richer our knowledge of God. For a beginning of our study of *is*, finite being lies ready to our hand, accessible, apt to our habits. It is only a shadow of infinite Being, but even a shadow is still something immense if infinite Being has cast it. Just as finite language is inadequate to express our knowledge, yet is the best we have and not to be spurned without loss, so finite being is an inadequate expression of infinite Being, yet is the best we have as a starting point and can yield immense fruit of knowledge.

III

We must study being, not simply as a philosophical concept, but as a reality expressed in everything that exists. We shall do better if we arrive at our own mental relation with being from our own experience of the things that are, and not simply from books in which other men abstract for us the fruit of theirs. Certainly it would be folly to think that we are likely to get a better notion of infinite Being by ignoring finite being. For in the first place, as we have seen, it bears at its lowest the imprint, and at its highest the likeness, of its Maker. It would be a singular aberration to think one could learn nothing about God from the things he has made—from the heavens, for example, which show forth God's glory.

The mind really aware of the splendour of creation cannot but feel how superb must be the infinite Being, if he can make this admirable stuff out of nothing. It is no compliment to God's omnipotence to treat what he has made of nothing as if it were little better than nothing. It is no compliment to a poet to be always seeking him and resolutely refusing to read his poetry. God *is* communicating with us, telling us something, by way of his universe. There is something verging on the monstrous about knowing God and not being interested in the things he has made, the things in which his infinite power is energizing. The logical development of so strange an attitude would be to love God so exclusively that we could not love men—an exclusiveness which he has forbidden. We have to love our neighbour because God loves him, and love demands knowledge. We cannot at once love our neighbour and ignore him; and we have to love the world, because God loves the world; and coming to know the world, we find that we are knowing God better. Provided that we keep the proportion right, our relation to God is better and richer because of our use, with mind and will and body, of what He has made.

But note again: in its way the created universe *is*, and from it we can get a real if quite unsayable notion of what *is* means. But as our knowledge grows, we are conscious of a kind of two-way effect —a growing sense of the wonder of it, and a growing awareness of the element of nothingness in it. As against not-being, nothing, it is so measurelessly great. As against Infinity, it barely is at all.

Given that the created universe has to be studied, how shall we study it? There is no one set way. Once one has the shape of reality, there is almost no way of *not* studying it, if one's mind is not abnormally lethargic. Once one has the main elements of reality clear in the mind, everything can add to the richness. Indeed a great deal of the enriching process will be spontaneous and unmeditated. We have not to be for ever setting our teeth and working con-scientiously at the enrichment of our mind. Direct study of the universe there must be, but it will not be the whole of the mind's action or the best part of it. Any living activity will serve. There is, for example, an immense amount to be learned about being, and therefore about God if one knows how to apply it, merely by having a cold plunge on a winter morning.

IV

On the same principle of learning from our own experience in living, there is much to be learned by sharing the fruit of the experience of others by reading—not simply reading philosophy, but the works of men especially gifted to react to reality. The theologian may well have something to gain from the novelist. For if the novelist has only a vague notion or no notion at all of the total meaning of life, he has usually a highly developed awareness of the flesh and blood of it. But far more than novels, the theologian might gain by reading the poets—and not only because they might improve his style, though this is more important than he always realizes. In that *awareness* of reality which is so vital, the poet really has something to give the theologian.

Wordsworth's

> The moon doth with delight
> Look round her when the heavens are bare

and Virgil's "*Sunt lachrymae rerum*" witness over eighteen hundred years to the same truth: the poets cannot be happy with the idea that nature is dead. They feel the life in it, though they do not always know what the life is that they feel. The Christian is exactly the reverse: he knows what the mystery is, but for the most part does not feel it. He knows as a fact of Christian doctrine that God is at the very centre of all things whatsoever, sustaining them by his own continuing life above the surface of that nothingness from which he drew them: but he does not experience things that way. What the Christian knows as a truth, the poet responds to as a living fact: he see things so. That is the one half of his gift. By the other half, he can communicate his experience, so that we see them so, too. Thus the poet can help many men who know a great deal more about creation than he does. He can help them by making creation come alive to them.

But as we have said there is need of direct study of the created universe. Consider matter first. The natural sciences serve the lesser purpose of helping to make the world more habitable and the greater purpose of increasing our knowledge of it. This order of values is not simply a fad of my own. The scientist himself holds it. Science is from the Latin verb *scire*, to know. Science does not mean doing, it means knowing. We have the electric light, not because scientists wanted to give us a handier illuminant than gas, but because they wanted to know more about the nature of light and the nature of electricity. The handy-men may hang around the scientist, seeing how they can put to use what he discovers; but it is he that discovers, not they. And he is driven on to his discoveries by a passionate desire to know. But for him, and that quality in him, the handy-men would be helpless.

It would be startling, we have shown, for a theologian to think he could learn nothing about God from the things God made—any of them, therefore the material things too. The scientist has information to give the theologian which the theologian can turn to gold. The scientist is not as such a theologian. He is dealing with causes and arrangements and relations less fundamental than the First Cause and the First Principle of Order. Further, he keeps within the field of material things. Therefore *as a scientist* he does not and cannot know what it is all about. He can know an incredible amount about the things upon which he specializes, but from his science he cannot learn the totality of being and therefore he cannot know the full meaning, or any large part of the meaning, even of what he does know. He knows it out of its context. To give an illustration: the scientist who is only a scientist is in the position of a man who should have made a most detailed study of a human eye, never having seen a human face. The scientist is dealing with the relations of material things to one another and this is valid and valuable knowledge, requiring its own sort of asceticism and devotion. But it is very bad for him if he confines himself exclusively to it, for a scientist is also a man with a man's need to know and a man's capacity to know, the meaning of his own life. Nothing is valueless that God has made, but the things the scientist studies are the lowest in value; and apart from their relation to God and to the higher things of that creation which in their lowliness they complete, they would be of no value at all: this is how he tends to study them. To be engaged so closely in their study that larger realities remain unseen is to neglect the better part of his own humanity. No amount of excellence as a scientist can compensate for stuntedness and crippledness as a man. Yet these brilliant workers upon the lowest things may well be compensated by the good God for the blindness so many of them inflicted upon themselves.

The scientist loses more by not leaning from the theologian than the theologian loses by not learning from the scientist: in any event the theologian has never ignored the stuff of the universe as the scientist has ignored the mind behind the universe. The theologian can hardly help knowing that bread nourishes, that poison kills, that sex perturbs. But if one loses less than the other, both lose. The scientist's loss is not here our concern, but the theologian's is, since we are taking out first steps along his road. He and we can learn from all the things that bear God's imprint, but still more from those higher things that he made in his likeness— angels and the souls of men. There is more to be learned from studying angels, but not by us. Man lies more immediately to our hand. We can study him more conveniently than we can study the angels. We can study him not only in psychology classrooms or history classrooms, but in the workshop, the bus, the shaving mirror. The stupidest couplet that Alexander Pope ever wrote is:

> Know thou thyself, presume not God to scan,
> The proper study of man kind is man.

In divorcing the study of God from the study of man

Alexander Pope was wrong both ways; for man is a most excellent starting point for our study of the illimitable, while man cannot be understood apart from his relation to the illimitable, that is out of his context.

V

One is at first startled to be told that only in the Mystical Body can man be fully and satisfactorily himself. The real difficulty about the doctrine of the Mystical Body, it could be said, is not to grasp it but to believe that the Church really means it. It is not hard to believe in the Catholic Church as an organization established by Christ to which its members go for Christ's gifts of life and truth; but, about the idea of the Church as an organism into which we are built that we may live in the full stream of Christ's life as members of Christ, there is an extraordinariness which dazzles or baffles by seeming so utterly out of scale with us. The ordinary Catholic's first reaction, on being told that that is his condition in the Church, is an incredulous "What, me!" He feels not only that the thing is beyond his powers, but that it is rather beyond his desires. Our meagreness would have been satisfied— even, as we feel in this first reaction, better satisfied —by something less. Some less ardent context, we feel, would suit our ordinariness better.

We have already considered this difficulty in the mind. Here we may look at it again from a rather

different angle. Man must grasp that man is extraordinary. He is extraordinary like all creatures—
there is nothing prosaic about being held in existence
out of one's native nothingness by the continuing
will of Omnipotence; but he is more extraordinary
than other creatures, both by what God made him
and by what he has made of himself.

Let us consider ourselves a little. We are made
from nothing, but we are not made for nothing and
will never return into nothing. Without God we
should be nothing, but we are not without him and
will never be without him. He made us not only
into something, but into something that is like
him; and again not only into something that is like
him, but into something that he could himself
become, something that he thought enough of to
die for. Spiritual and immortal, made in the likeness
of God, redeemed by Christ, we are clustered with
splendours. Consider man's glory as we know it
against the dreariness of man as the atheist thinks
him. We have nothing as our origin, but eternity as
our destiny; the atheist has a cloud about his origin,
but nothing as his destiny. We come from nothing,
he is going to nothing. Fortunately his thinking so
does not make it so. Eternity will have surprises for
him, too.

In any event never think that the way of man is
prosaic. We are a mixture of matter and spirit, and
in this resemble no other creature—at least in the
universe known to us: of possible inhabitants of
other planets I know as little as the rest of men. We

are the only things who die and do not stay dead:
it seems an odd way to our goal that as the last stage
on the way to it all of us, saint and sinner, should
fall apart. We are the only beings with an everlasting
destiny who have not reached their final state. By
comparison there is something cosy and settled
about angels, good and bad. Men are the only beings
whose destiny is uncertain.

There is an effect of this in our consciousness,
if we choose to analyse it. There is a two-way drag
in all of us, and nothing could be more actual and
less academic than this curious fact. How actual it is
we can see if we compare our knowledge that the
planet we live on is not anchored in space. This
ought to be, one would think, the first thing we
should be aware of, yet it was only a few centuries
ago that scientists arrived at it; and most of us still
have to take the word of scientists for it. No one of
us has ever felt the whizz of the world through
space and the counter-drag of whatever power it is
that keeps us upon the earth's surface. But we *do*
feel the almost continuous drag in ourselves down-
wards towards nothingness and the all too occasional
upward thrust. Man is the cockpit of a battle. We
are the only creatures who can choose their side and
change their side in this battle. We are the only
beings left who can either choose or refuse God.
All the excitement of our universe is centred in man.

For we human beings started extraordinary, and
from extraordinary have grown monstrous—body
rebelling against soul, imagination playing the devil

with intellect, passion storming will. The medieval travellers' stories of men with their heads under their shoulders were not unjustly felt to be pretty startling. But men with their intellects under their imaginations and their wills under their passions are more startling still. The only reason we are not startled is that we are more sensitive to the shape, and therefore to any misshapenness, of body than of soul. Whatever other reasons we might have or think we have for rejecting the doctrine of the Mystical Body, let us not think of ourselves as too ordinary for so marvellous a context. No context could be too extraordinary for creatures like men.

VI

But the extraordinariness of both is not the only link between man and the Church. At every point in the nature of man the Church fits it. We may summarize the truth about all men in two pairs of facts: first, man is at once spirit and matter; second, he is at once an individual person and a social being. In each pair the Church sees both elements.

As to the first pair, the church makes such provision for the needs and powers of the soul as are undreamed of elsewhere; but the body is fully realized, too, by way of asceticism fitting it for full partnership with the soul, by way of sacrament and sacramental fitting it for companionship to the very furthest point the soul can go. Within the Church there is a consecration of soul and body, an awareness of sacredness in soul and body.

As to the second pair, the Church has turned the social element in man's nature to the uses of religion beyond any other church, seeing man united with his fellows in relation to God, uniting with his fellows in the worship of God, receiving God's gifts of truth and life through the fellowship. Yet the person remains himself, not merged in the human society here or in the divine nature hereafter, under God an end in himself, not a pawn in a game. Nowhere can a man more fully feel at once his kinship with all men and the worth of his own personality.

In relation to both our key facts, notice the two tides that have beaten on the Church in these last centuries, Protestantism and Secularism. Just as in each the Church preserved both components, so in each its assailants chose one component and let the other go. Protestantism stressed the soul and the individual. Secularism stressed the body and society. Consider these a little more closely.

Protestantism, we say, opted for the soul and largely ignored the body, or at least made no provision for it. It ruled out asceticism, most of the sacraments and all the sacramentals. It produced a religion for the soul only, which would have been well enough had man been a soul only, but was no religion for man. With the onrush of Secularism, the ignored element had its revenge. Secularism concentrated on the body, ignoring the spirit as completely as Protestantism ignored the body. Its aims are primarily the body's good, comfort and security, on the general assumption that, if man does happen to have a soul, it will be satisfied by improved material conditions. The result is the starvation of the spirit.

Again the emphasis of Protestantism was on the relation of the individual soul to God, any co-operation of man being regarded as an intrusion. There is a truth in this, but it is not the whole truth. There is an element in man beyond the reach of his fellows, something incommunicable which must have its own unshared relation with God, but that element is not the whole of man, and the effort to build the whole of religion upon it as if it were, means ultimately that even it does not reach its fullest achievement. It is within the Catholic Church that mysticism has reached its most marvellous point, as indeed the spiritual non-Catholic shows by reading the works of our mystics in preference to his own. There is the same revenge of the ignored element here as earlier. Secularism came, betting everything upon the social order as aginst the human person. We see this at its logical extreme in Communism and Fascism, where the collective is everything and the individual has literally no meaning and certainly no destiny apart from it. But though in these two the tendency has gone furthest, the same tendency runs through all modern sociology. The only home left for personality is the Church. Only for the Church is everyone someone.

Thus both Protestantism and Secularism maim man by treating him as half of himself. The Church alone treats man as the whole of himself in the whole of his context.

VII

But if the Church gives us the whole truth in perfect balance, there is a danger that we, receiving it thus whole and balanced, may not use our own minds sufficiently upon it. It is a great thing to preserve truth inviolate, but less so if one keeps it unexamined. And within this danger there is the subtler danger of thinking one's mind active upon the truth when one is in fact merely exercising it upon words. In this matter of what man is, the Catholic is in real danger of stopping at the words of the definition as though knowing them were equivalent to knowing man.

Man, says the philosopher, is a rational animal. He is indeed. As a definition, the phrase is perfect; but as a description it would be totally inadequate. The object of a definition is to define, that is to make a statement about a thing which will apply to that thing exclusively. It is a pointer which points to one single thing, the thing it defines. The phrase "rational animal" manages to point at *man* and at nothing else within our experience: the word "animal" cuts out every being that is not animal; the word "rational" cuts out every animal that is not man. The phrase distinguishes man from the

29

octopus, say, and from the angel (just as the derisive phrase "unfeathered biped" distinguishes him from bird and beast, since no beast is biped and no bird unfeathered). Once one has put enough into the definition to exclude every other thing, to add anything further would be superfluous. But this means that there is far more in anything than its definition tells. Too many treat the phrase rational animal or the alternative phrase "union of spirit and matter" as a sort of blackboard diagram upon which they proceed to base their thinking on the affairs of man. But in fact either phrase is too meagre a foundation. It leaves out too much—the fact, for instance, that man is fallen.

The truth is that no book and no statement by someone else can tell us what man is. Only life can do that. Every man one meets can add to our knowledge of what man is, provided that we know how to learn. If we want really to understand man, it is not enough to study animality and rationality, on the principle of the man in *Pickwick Papers* who, having to write an article on Chinese Metaphysics, looked up China in the encyclopaedia, then Metaphysics, and combined the information. If you want to find out what a rational animal is, study man; neither animality nor rationality will be the same when the two are wed: the marriage does strange things to both of them. Rationality functioning in union with a body is not just rationality; animality is so ennobled by its marriage with spirit that no mere animal would know what to do with it. The way to find all this is to meet man and think hard about the experience.

As an example of the mass of actuality that can be wrapped up in a phrase, consider some of the first things that experience shows, and the phrase does not in itself tell us, about man as a union of spirit and matter. The word "union" is a word with a vast variety of meanings. If one is content with the word without getting at the one special meaning which applies to man, then one will never know what man is at all, and this would be a pity since it means a profound ignorance about oneself. Not to know what an angel is is a misfortune; not to know what a man is threatens sanity.

Let us glance at our phrase, beginning with the word union. The union is of two beings one of them spatial, one of them spaceless. Two unlikelier beings for a union it would be hard to conceive If we had not the fact of it under our noses, we should be inclined to think that if any union were possible between two such, it could be only a very sketchy and casual union. But the fact is that these two beings are united so closely that they constitute one being, one person, one subsistent operative thing. We have already considered the union in a rather abstract way, but it may be worth repeating something of what has been said and adding some further points.

We have here a union of flame and water, the flame enflaming every part of the water, so that the water is immeasurably different from water unflamed both in what it is and in what it can do; so in the human compound, the body acted on by a spiritual soul is immeasurably different from a merely animal body. If ever there were a water and a flame, so related that that flame could heat only that water and that water be heated by no flame but that, we should have a figure closer still. For the soul of man and the body of man can in the one case give and in the other case receive the lifegiving energy only in relation to each other. My soul could not animate your body. In the most literal sense a man's soul and body are made for one another.

A union so close, and here the figure of the flame and the water becomes totally inadequate, might be expected to affect the soul in its own proper activities. And so we find it. There is not only that border region of emotion and passion where it is hard to tell which is more in operation, but, in the activity of intellectual knowledge, which is the soul's own special affair and for which the body as such has no competence at all, the body does in fact play a part. The soul receives all that information upon the outside world—upon which it does its own thinking and from which it draws knowledge amounting ultimately to the knowledge of God Himself— through the doorways of the body's senses. While soul and body maintain their union here upon earth, the body must play this organic part in the soul's knowing, or the soul not know.

The inter-relation of soul and body in the concrete living of life is the commonest fact of experience.

States of the soul produce effects upon the body. What happens to the body produces states of the soul. And all this Protestantism chooses to ignore. At any rate it will not be ignorable in Heaven. We have observed that the flame can go on flaming even after the water is taken away. And the soul can continue in its own spiritual activities even after the body has reached a point where it can no longer respond to the animating energies of the soul and we have the separation which is called death. But the separation is not to be permanent. For this immeasurably close union constitutes the fullness of man. And man's ultimate destiny is to live the life of Heaven not as part of himself, even the noblest part, but as his whole self.

VIII

We have glanced a little at the union of spirit and matter; we may now look at its other face, the union of rationality and animality. At first sight these two look if anything less apt for life together than "spaceless" and "spatial". In terms of marriage it looks like the most impossible mésalliance. Friendly angels may well have shaken their heads and malicious devils rubbed their hands to see a marriage that looked so certain to go on the rocks, and which very soon looked as if it had in fact gone on the rocks. Rationality and animality are so oddly assorted in themselves that they seemed to need ideal circum-

33

stances to give them any chance, and ideal circum-
stances are just what they did not get, at least for
long. In our own experience we know how bother-
some a union it is. An archangel or a cat would be
driven mad in twenty-four hours by the problem
of living in two such various worlds at once. Indeed
madness sometimes looks like a pretty good sum-
marization of what man has made of the problem
himself, a madness we have got used to.

The trouble is that animality is so much easier
than rationality. For one thing it is quite effortless,
whereas rationality demands effort. We are good at
animality and very much attached to it: we find
rationality difficult and not so immediately rewarding.
What makes it worse is that the soul can enjoy the
body's pleasures as the body cannot enjoy the soul's.
The dice seem heavily loaded in favour of animality,
especially in a generation as fatigued as ours. Yet
we *have* spiritual and not only animal needs. The
body is on the quest, but the spirit is on the quest,
too. The body quests more clamorously, but the
spirit is never wholly silent, and its hungers can be
as real and even as torturing as the body's. We shall
see more of these hungers of the soul, but pause
here long enough to grant their reality. The soul can
enjoy the body's satisfactions, but it cannot be
satisfied with them. There is a trouble in it, and an
unawareness of what is troubling it. H. G. Wells
half hit it in his description of one of his heroes—
"a street arab in love with unimaginable god-
desses".

34

There is a conflict in man between these two so different sets of needs and the result is a kind of near chaos. Rationality and animality either complete each other (and that if the relation is exactly right), or perturb each other, neither knowing what is the matter. They tend to fissure, making two beings of us instead of one: but two incomplete beings. The needs of the body inflame the soul; and the needs of the soul torment the whole man in such a way as to mar the perfection of the body's pleasure in its pleasure, and the animality is spurred further to provide what it cannot provide, namely satisfaction for the whole man; and so we get every sort of perversion and that sort of depravity which in our exasperation we call animal, but which is not animal at all and would shock an animal to the root of his being if he could comprehend it; and mixed with the perversion and the depravity strange streaks of magnificence. Chaos is the only word, and if we are not aware of the chaos, then we do not know man. The chaos roars or mutters or only whimpers, according to the energy of the man and what he has made of the conflict. It may be only a kind of uneasy shifting or sense of insecurity. But it must always be taken into account.

The fact of this conflict within man is one reason why we should not judge other men. Our Lord tells us not to judge, "lest we be judged". That is one reason, but it is not the only reason. We should refrain from judgment not only because we expose ourselves to judgment, but because we have not the knowledge that judgment needs. The quick slick confident judgments we are for ever making are merely silly. Who can read the chaos in another's soul from which his actions proceed? Who can read the chaos in his own soul?

IX

What we have just seen is simply a sample of what beginners in the study of man can find out for themselves on their way to deeper knowledge. Such a study once entered upon must not be allowed to cease. We must keep on studying man. We may not be able to say, that is to cast into words, the new knowledge we gain; but there is an intimacy, a new feel and instinct for man such as a good sculptor gets for stone, which will make the most enormous difference to our handling of all men, and especially of the man who is ourself. Each must make the study for himself. But we may summarize here two of the things that will become always clearer. The first is that man is incalculable. Man is a rational animal. But that does not mean that he is a reasonable animal. It means only that he has reason, and therefore can misuse it. If he had not reason, he could not be unreasonable. But he has, and is. That is what I mean by his incalculability. But once you have said that man is incalculable, you have said that the definition is not enough, that no definition could be enough, and indeed no description. We must never take our eye off him: he is always liable to surprise us, and himself, too.

The second truth is that man is insufficient for himself, not only by the ill use he has made of himself, but in any event. There must be clarity here. So many of our troubles flow from a defective use of the intelligence or will or energy we have, that we are in danger of thinking that all our troubles could be cured by a better use of our own powers—in other words that man has the secret of sufficiency within himself if he will but use it. But apart from failings that we can do something about, there is a radical insufficiency in us flowing altogether from our being. Man is insufficient without God because without God he would not even be. It is easy for man to think himself autonomous, if he does not think very much: for God does not jerk his elbow, so to speak, but only solicits his mind. But that a being who does not bring himself into existence and who cannot put himself out of existence should think that it is by any power of his own that he is maintained in existence in a sign that his mind must be engaged upon other matters. For fullness of being, man must have a knowledge of and a co-operation with that which maintains him in existence, that which is the very condition of his be-ing at all. To be wrong about that, is to be wrong about oneself—to see oneself as one is not, to act as one is not, to aim at what is not (which means loving things for what they are not). There is an abyss of nothingness at the very heart of our being, and we had better counter it by the fullest possible use of our kinship with the Infinite who is also at the very heart of our being. To be ignorant of this is to live in unreality, and there can be no satisfaction for ourself or any adequate coping with anything.

2. Born of a Woman

"Mary figured profoundly in the history of salvation and in a certain way unites and mirrors within herself the central truths of the faith. Hence when she is being preached and venerated, she summons the faithful to her Son and his sacrifice, and to love for the Father. . . . The Virgin Mary in her own life lived an example of that maternal love by which all should be fittingly animated who cooperate in the apostolic mission of the Church on behalf of the rebirth of men."—*Dogmatic Constitution on the Church* VIII, 3, 65.

"God sent his Son, born of a woman," Paul told the Galatians. Paul's "dear physician" Luke, who tells the story thus summarized, begins his Gospel: "Many have taken in hand to set forth in order a narration of the things that have been accomplished among us, according as those have delivered them to us who from the beginning were eye-witnesses and ministers of the Word. So it seemed good to me also, having carefully [*akribōs*] investigated all things from the beginning, to write to you, in order, most excellent Theophilus, that you may know the truth of those words in which you have been instructed."

The Greek word *akribōs*—it means carefully, accurately—could hardly have prepared Theophilus for what follows immediately—the angel Gabriel bringing to the priest Zechariah the announcement that his elderly wife would bear his elderly self a son; the angel going on to tell a virgin in Nazareth that she would conceive. One imagines Theophilus muttering *akribōs* to himself—all the more if he had known Luke as a pagan in his medical student days at Tarsus.

An angel was well enough as ornament, fancy scrollwork in the margin as it were. But what was it doing after that sort of introductory guarantee of careful investigation? Had it been a matter of Socrates and his *daimōn*—Plato said each man had one—Theophilus would have known where he was. The daimon was more an influence than a person, but this angel was not like that. He belonged with those superhuman messengers in human form, sent by gods to men, with whom Greek mythology was littered. All that was behind Theophilus, he and his sort had long outgrown it.

Gabriel must have bothered him, as he still bothers people. He does not, of course, bother those who do not believe in angels, they simply reject him out of hand. But many, whose religion tells them that angels really exist, are yet uncomfortable with them, wish they would keep their distance, feel that this particular story would be tidier without Gabriel. What need for an angel? God could have given Mary the explanation of her pregnancy without using an angel, they say—just as there are those who say God can give sinners forgiveness without using a priest.

A second problem for Theophilus would surely have been the curious Greek of the opening chapters. Luke's own language was Greek, and the rest of his Gospel shows that he wrote it rather well. Then why two chapters of such very un-Greek Greek? This may have been the first question Theophilus asked Luke: "What language do you think you're writing?"

Luke's first answer may have been that he was not the author—that apart from a few touches, he simply used the account he had received, either already translated into Greek, or in Aramaic to be translated by himself. From whom had he received it? Ultimately from our Lady, perhaps through St John (to whose Gospel his own has so many likenesses). So careful an investigator would not have failed to question the Apostle to whose sonship her own Son had committed her. He must have had many opportunities, if only in the two years he seems to have spent in Caesarea, forty miles from Jerusalem, while Paul was a prisoner there.

Mary, Luke says, was betrothed to a man called Joseph. Of him we know very little. Did he, like Mary, belong to Nazareth at the time of the betrothal? Scripture does not say. He was a carpenter, and he had in him the noblest blood that Israel knew, for he was a descendant of King David. Why should a man of that lineage have been a carpenter? We know that the house of David had fallen into obscurity, and obscurity and poverty were practically interchangeable terms. In the great revolt led by the Maccabees, which gave the Jews their last breath of independence before Rome swallowed them, the sons of David played no conspicuous part. A century or so after this, when the Roman Emeror Domitian ordered the destruction of David's known descendants as possible centres of revolt against Roman rule, some at least were spared because they were so poor and insignificant that even the tyrant could not see them as a serious threat. It is all very puzzling to us, since we know that the Messiah, the expectation of Israel, was to be a son of David.

We are told that Joseph was of David's house. Was Mary? Again, Scripture is silent. Catholics, I think, take it for granted that she was. It is true that the Jews considered adoption as practically equivalent to physical generation: the acknowledgement by Joseph of Jesus as his child would have been legally sufficient to make Jesus a son of David. But the language of the New Testament seems to demand for our Lord something more than a merely legal descent from David. In his first great sermon, St Peter speaks of Christ our Lord as "the fruit of David's loins" (Acts 2:30); St Paul speaks of him as "made of the seed of David, according to the flesh" (Rom 1:3). These would be strong terms for a purely legal relationship. We have no certain knowledge, but there is something attractive in the idea, proposed by many scholars, that St Joseph was a close relation of our Lady, so that her ancestry would be largely his.

Betrothal, for the Jews of that day, was not simply an engagement to marry. After betrothal, the couple were husband and wife. Each continued to live at home—for a year if the bride was a virgin, for a month if she was a widow. Then came the wedding celebrations and the solemn entry of the bride into her husband's house. In the period

44

between, the marriage act would have been unusual, but not sinful. For the couple were husband and wife.

Mary of Nazareth came pregnant to the wedding, though the marriage act had not taken place. If we knew no more than this—that she, still a virgin, found herself by God's will pregnant—we should feel that she was at least entitled to an explanation: and only God could give it. It is Luke who tells how God gave it. And it was not an explanation after the fact. Before the child was, by a miracle of God's power, conceived of her, Luke tells of explanation from God and consent from her. The child, our Saviour and hers, was not forced upon her.

Message to Mary

Six months after the visit to Zechariah in the Temple in Jerusalem, Gabriel was sent by God to Mary in her own town of Nazareth. Did the angel appear, visibly I mean? Luke does not say so this time, though he does say that Zechariah saw him. Unless the reader knows St Luke's account word by word almost, he should read Luke 1:26–38 before going on to what is written here. Few as the verses are they contain the longest conversation anyone is recorded by Scripture as having with our Blessed Lady—she actually speaks twice! Luke's statement is so perfect that one's first feeling is that not a word need be added. Yet without commentary we shall miss a great deal of what is there for us.

45

Gabriel's opening words are: "Hail, full of grace, the Lord is with thee; blessed art thou among women." Mary made no reply. Gabriel misunderstood her silence. Perhaps remembering Zechariah, he told her not to be afraid. Clearly he did not yet know her very well. Contact with Zechariah was no preparation at all for understanding Mary of Nazareth. Her silence was not from terror, but from perplexity—she was "much perplexed at hearing him speak so, and cast about in her mind what she was to make of such a greeting".

Only the opening word "Hail" would have given her no trouble (the Greek word, used by St Luke, meant Joy; the corresponding salutation in Hebrew was Peace). The next word, which we translate "full of grace", was a different matter. There is no record of its ever having been addressed to anyone else; nor, indeed, can we be sure of its precise meaning. The form of the verb carries the sense of abundance; but abundance of what? Of "charis", the Greek word tells us. That word has, ever since St Paul, meant sanctifying grace, and so it might have meant on the angel's lips; but it *might* have meant "privilege"—that she had been chosen by God for some great work. Whether it was grace or whether it was privilege, either way Mary had it in abundance. Either way she might well wonder.

The phrase that follows, "the Lord is with thee", was an immeasurable compliment. We ourselves say Good-bye, which means May God be with you. But what Gabriel said was not that. He was not

46

expressing a desire that God might be with her. He was stating as a fact that God *was* with her! To whom had a statement of *that* fact ever been made? Her Son was to promise to be with his whole Church until the end of time. But as we know, and Gabriel knew, it was about to have a meaning for Mary which it never had had for a human being before, and never could again.

Later we shall find Elizabeth saying "Blessed art thou among women". Most scholars think it is her phrase, not Gabriel's—a copyist inserted it here in error. Wherever Mary heard it, it would have perplexed her, not as the other two phrases did because the words were unfamiliar, but because they were not. She had met them before! They are applied in the Old Testament to two women. One of them was Jael, who had saved God's people by hammering a tent peg into the skull of the enemy leader, Sisera (Judges 4). The other was Judith, who had saved God's people by cutting the head off the enemy leader Holophernes (Judith 13). A young girl might well have been startled at a compliment, however splendid in itself, which linked her with these particular heroines of her people. She did not know, as we know and Gabriel knew, that she was to bear a Son who would crush a mightier and more malignant head than Sisera had or Holophernes.

None of the puzzling things Gabriel had so far said to Mary of Nazareth was any preparation for what he said next.

"Thou shalt conceive in thy womb, and shalt bear a Son, and shalt call him Jesus. He shall be great, and men will know him for the Son of the Most High. The Lord God will give him the throne of his father David, and he shall reign over the house of Jacob eternally; his kingdom shall never have an end."

Even a very slight knowledge of the Old Testament would have made it clear to her that the son she was to conceive, the son to be called Jesus (which means "God saves"), was to be the Messiah. She may have recognized the words that the prophet Nathan had said long ago to David—"Thy throne shall remain forever" (2 Samuel 7:16); and the words of Isaiah, "He will sit on David's kingly throne, to give it lasting foundations of justice and right" (Isaiah 9:7); in any event the one thing every Jew knew was that the Messiah was to be son of David. But could she yet have known the meaning of the phrase "Son of the Most High"? Only if the doctrine of the Blessed Trinity had been specially revealed to her, as it is not revealed in the Old Testament.

"Thou shalt conceive"—but when? The future tense can be used for anything from the next minute to the end of the world. Catholics believe that the Annunication and the conception of Christ in his mother's womb belong together. The Church, celebrating Christ's birth on 25 December, celebrates the Annunciation exactly nine months before, on 25 March.

Zechariah, told of a son to be conceived, had

been incredulous and had asked for a sign. Mary was not incredulous, she asked for no sign. She simply asked how—"How shall this be done, because I know not man?" This particular use of the verb to know comes very early in Scripture—"Adam knew Eve his wife: and she conceived and brough forth Cain." Our Lady is asking how she can conceive since she is still a virgin.

Gabriel answered: "The Holy Spirit will come upon thee, and the power of the Most High will overshadow thee. Thus the Holy which shall be born of thee shall be called Son of God."

Mary's question is completely answered. The child was not to be conceived, as she herself had been conceived, in the usual way of marriage. That which, in any conception, is provided by the mother, she would provide. But what in every other conception the father provides would in this one case be produced by a miracle of God's power. The conception was to be virginal, an idea for which the Old Testament (with its absence of virgins) had no more prepared her than pagan mythology (with its absence of virgin births) would later prepare Theophilus.

Our Lady said: "Behold the handmaid of the Lord; be it done to me according to thy word"— words of consecration bringing the Second Person of the Blessed Trinity into her womb, into our race. Why had she held her acceptance of God's will unspoken until this moment? Not because she had to be persuaded. God's will was sufficient for her—

49

she actually used a stronger word than "handmaid"; she said: "Behold the slave of the Lord." She waited before uttering her consent, surely, because she felt that if God sent her a message she owed it to him to understand it.

Through the ages there has been a tendency among those who love Jesus to concentrate on, and magnify, the differences between him and other men to the point where his humanness hardly matters. No heresy has a more continuous appeal to the devout than the earliest of all, Docetism, with its teaching that his human body was only a phantom.

The tendency is the other way today. Yet there are still those who see any serious emphasis on his manhood and its limitations as a denial of his divinity. There is a simplification in *either* man *or* God that only heads clear enough for the rich complexity of *both* man *and* God can avoid.

We begin with the error already referred to— that his body was new-made for him with all the perfections a human body can have. This would mean that his body was not conceived by Mary, but that an embryo, not drawn from her body but created by God independently of it, was placed in her womb that it might make use of the womb's facilities for the necessary nine months (there were indeed early heretics who held this). She would have been the baby's hostess, not his mother.

Against this stand the statements of Matthew and Luke that she conceived him. Peter has told us that he was the fruit of David's loins (Acts 2:30),

Paul that he was of the seed of David according to the flesh. So, naturally, was his mother. She received sanctifying grace, the Church has defined, at the moment of her conception; but this did not replace her genes and chromosomes. Christ's ancestry then, like ours, goes back to the origin of the human race. He got his body, as we get ours, from a myriad ancestors—back 35,000 years? 350,000? how many? This, as we have already noted, was the body in which he died for our redemption and rose again. More to our present purpose, it was the body he had to live with, to cope with; the cross often enough that he had to carry, as we have to carry ours.

The Word Made Flesh

The conception announced by the angel Gabriel concerned two persons principally—the Mother and the Son. There is not one of us, of course, whom it does not concern more deeply than anything else that ever happened; but these two principally. St Luke, in the beginning of his Gospel, concentrates upon the Mother. St John, in the beginning of his, treats wholly of the Son: the Mother indeed is there, but not by direct reference. What St John tells us of the Son makes the words of Gabriel, quoted by St Luke, dazzlingly, almost dazingly, clear. If we are neither dazed nor dazzled, it can only mean that we have not been listening!

Gabriel had said: "The Holy which shall be born of thee shall be called Son of God." In Hebrew

usage this meant that he would *be* Son of God—
God's messenger not having been sent to call
someone what he is not! What did the phrase Son
of God mean? We, taught by the Church Christ
founded, assume that Son of God meant God the
Son. But, in the first place, although the Old
Testament contains gleams and hints of the Blessed
Trinity, it does not actually teach the doctrine. And,
in the second place, the phrase "sons of God" is
used (by the prophet Hosea, for example) to mean
men who are in God's grace. It is quite clear that
Gabriel meant more than this. The Holy Ghost
should come upon her and the power of the Most
High should overshadow her—the Jews knew no
mightier words to express a special presence and
operation of God. Words of that splendour could not
mean merely that she would give birth to one more
Jew of true piety: that would have been total anti-
climax. Her child would be Son of God as no one
ever had been or ever would be. But in what would
that Sonship consist?

St John tells us. He does the actual conception
in one swift stroke—"The Word was made flesh
and dwelt among us." Then, in a phrase of total
clarity, he tells who the Word is— "And we saw
his glory, the glory as of the only-begotten of the
Father." Others had been called sons of God in the
Old Testament; a few phrases earlier, St John
himself has referred to men who become sons of
God by grace. But the Word was not of these; he
was the only-begotten; he did not become the Son

of God, he was born so, in the timelessness of eternity. Twice in this first chapter St John calls him the only-begotten; it is by the power of the only-begotten that the rest of men may be made sons of God.

St John begins by calling the only-begotten not the Son but the Word: "In the beginning was the Word [*logos*] and the Word was with God, and the Word was God." Never in the history of human speech has so much richness of reality been uttered with such brevity. All eternity will not be enough to unpack its content. God utters a Word, not a word made of air expelled from the lungs and shaped by throat and tongue and teeth and lips, for God is a spirit. It is not a word of the mouth but a word in the mind, an idea. We are given the truth about this idea in two steps. The Word has always been *with* God. The Word *is* God.

God, knowing himself with infinite knowing power, generates in the divine mind an idea of himself. We all have an idea of ourselves in our mind, not always a very accurate idea, even our dearest friends might laugh if they could know the idea we have of ourselves. But God's idea of himself is totally accurate, totally adequate. There is nothing in himself that is not in the idea that he eternally generates of himself; and whereas our idea is merely something, his is Someone as he himself is Someone, God as he is God. And this second Someone within the Godhead is eternal as he is eternal—there never was a moment when God did not thus see himself

53

imaged in his Son, there are no moments in eternity.

Thus the Son whom Mary conceived in her womb, the Son who received human nature in her womb, already possessed the divine nature eternally.

One might read a vast amount of discussion of "the Johannine logos" without realizing that John barely mentions the word (except of course, in its ordinary sense of "something said"). We might get the impression that John was wholly logos-minded, logos-soaked, perhaps converted to the logos in some Patmos vision, as totally possessed by it as Paul by his experience on the Damascus road. In fact John mentions it only twice (or three times, if he was the author of the Apocalypse); and he gives no indication of why he uses it at all: he never discusses the concept or draws anything from it. From Word he passes within a few verses to Son, and Son it remains for the rest of the Gospel. In the perspective of his Gospel as a whole, one wonders if he might not just as well have said "In the beginning was the Son, and the Son was with God, and the Son was God".

Why did John use the word if he was going to make no use of it, so to speak? We have already spoken of the use Christians have made of it from John's day to our own: we should have been hard put to it to give any meaning to God's having a Son, if we had not been able to think of the divine Mind conceiving a Word, in which the whole of the divine reality was uttered. Was John throwing light on the question how God could have a son?

We have been studying the conception of our Lord as St Luke tells it and as St John tells it. Before continuing let us summarize what we have learnt thus far about him. In the womb of Mary of Nazareth, through the nine months of gestation, was one who was fully human, but not solely human. The person, growing towards birth as every human baby grows, was the Second Person of the Blessed Trinity, God the Son. Mary was his mother. Possessing the divine nature eternally, he received a human nature of her: this one divine Person now had two natures. To his humanity she contributed all that our mothers contribute to ours. She was not simply the mother of his human nature, but of himself—as my mother is not the mother of my nature but of me. Mary was the mother of God the Son. That is what we learn from St John; that in more veiled language is what St Luke quotes Gabriel as telling her.

Mary visits Zechariah's Wife

St John and St Luke tell the story from two different points of view. One link between them is that both bring in John the Baptist. St John almost seems to interrupt what he is telling us of the Word, to say "There was a man sent from God, whose name was John . . . he was not the light but was to give testimony of the light." And when the verses which form the Prologue of the Gospel are ended St John turns immediately to the preaching of John the

55

Baptist. Similarly Gabriel, having delivered the supreme message, says to our Lady: "Thy cousin Elizabeth also has conceived a son in her old age . . . to prove that nothing can be impossible with God." Gabriel says nothing is impossible to God as a comment upon a woman past child-bearing. Jesus was to say the same thing thirty years later with reference to the rich entering heaven.

As the Angel departed Mary, "went into the hill country with haste to visit Elizabeth". We tend to think of the Visitation as the meeting of the two mothers. But far more important was the meeting of the two sons. When Elizabeth heard her cousin's greeting, "the infant leaped in her womb". What this first meeting of the Redeemer and his fore-runner, each in the womb of his mother, meant to either of them, we have no earthly means of knowing. But there is a kind of excitement in it for us—which is not diminished when we learn that the Greek verb for John's "leaping" is the same as for David's (2 Samuel 6:14–16) when he danced before the Ark of the Lord—a wooden chest containing the written word of God. Our Lady was far more truly the Ark of the Lord than the one made by Moses ever was— though it, too, had been overshadowed by the power of the Most High. It was not the written Word of God that she had within her.

Elizabeth's opening words are: "Blessed are thou among women and blessed is the fruit of thy womb." But two other things Elizabeth says upon which we must linger for a moment.

56

The first is "How have I deserved to be thus visited by the mother of my Lord?" Here the word "Lord" means at least Messiah. But in the Septuagint, the Greek translation of the Old Testament, the word was used for God; and although Elizabeth had probably never read the Septuagint, she had a special reason for using this word in the same sense—for Gabriel had said to Zechariah that her son should "convert many of the children of Israel to the *Lord* their *God*." Zechariah was certainly in her mind when she uttered the second of the phrases upon which we thus briefly linger—"Blessed art thou for thy believing"—for Zechariah still suffered from the dumbness which had come upon him because of his failure to believe.

When Mary spoke, it was not to Elizabeth. The Magnificat is a cry . . . a cry to God and to all men. It is woven of passages from the Old Testament, especially the prayer that Anna had prayed at the birth of Samuel (1 Samuel 2:1–10). If that prayer is not familiar to you, do please read it and then re-read the Magnificat. The similarities are obvious, the differences more so.

There is one phrase of Anna which we cannot imagine on our Lady's lips—"Now can I flout my enemies!" And there are so many phrases in the Magnificat which could never have sounded on any lips but hers. Greatest of these is "All generations shall call me blessed". Spoken by a girl in her teens, from an insignificant townlet in Galilee, bride of a carpenter, the claim might seem monstrous: more so even than the promise made later by that other carpenter, her Son, that he would build his Church upon a fisherman and the gates of hell should not prevail against it. Either claim really would have been monstrous—if it had not been fulfilled.

Even to those who know that all generations *have* called her blessed, there is a kind of surprise in the way Mary links a statement of so much glory to her "humility" (better, her lowliness). Here again there is an echo of something her Son was to say— "Learn of me, *because* I am meek and humble of heart."

Certainly there is no self-glorification in the Magnificat. In the reference to her humility we find her, in our English version, once more calling herself "handmaid" as she did to Gabriel, and once more St Luke's Greek word means "slave". The word startles us. We are more startled still to hear her, whose soul was filled with grace at the moment of her conception and never stained by sin, call God her Saviour. There is a vast theological reality here. God was truly her Saviour, both because by his power she was conceived in sanctifying grace and saved from ever sinning; and because, sinless though she was, she was still a member of a sinful race—a race to which heaven was closed until the Saviour healed the breach between it and God.

Born of a Woman

Message to Joseph

The two most immediately concerned in the conception of Christ were the Mother and the Son. Luke has told us of one, John of the other. But there was a third, Joseph, very differently but most deeply concerned: for his wife conceived a child, of which he was not the father. Matthew tells of him (1:18–25).

Joseph's discovery and his reaction to it Matthew gives in about forty close-packed words. Let us begin to unpack them. We shall not see the greatness of Joseph if we simply read them and pass swiftly on: and that was surely Matthew's reason for telling us the episode at all.

Mary was betrothed to Joseph; they had not yet begun their life together. Betrothal, as we have noted, was not with the Jews simply an engagement to marry, it was marriage. The ceremony—as we know it to have been somewhat later and as it may well have been in the time of Mary and Joseph—was very simple. Its elements are still to be found in our own marriage ceremonial. In the presence of two competent witnesses, the man handed the woman a coin—the smallest would do—or some token gift instead: and he said "Be thou consecrated to me". The husband and wife did not set up house together at once, she remained with her family, he with his. But husband and wife they were. In this first chapter we find Matthew calling Joseph "husband", the angel calling Mary "wife".

And now Mary "was found to be with child". Between the betrothal and the wife's entry into her husband's house as we have noted, the marriage act was not customary among the Jews. But if it did take place—which it rarely did in Galilee, more often in Judea—it was not sinful, and a child born of it was legitimate.

How did Joseph learn that Mary was to bear a child? We remember her "Be it done into me according to thy word"—addressed, one imagines, not to Gabriel but to God direct. She had gone immediately after saying it to Elizabeth in Judea. Three months later she was back in Nazareth. Some time after that it would have been evident that she was to have a child. The women of Nazareth would have noticed; and they would instantly have told their husbands. Did one of the husbands remark on it to Joseph? Whoever told him, we can feel sure that Joseph received the news in silence. He was a silent man; and, in any event, what could he say?

Why had Mary not told Joseph herself? We do not know. We do not even know where Joseph was living at the time of Gabriel's visit to Mary. He may have been in some other town of Galilee or even in Judea—we remember that when later they returned from Egypt their first intention was to settle in Judea. Mary may not have seen him after the Annunciation. Would she, in any event, have found it so simple to tell him? She may well have felt it was for God to tell Joseph, as he had told herself.

"Joseph her husband, being a just man and not

willing publicly to expose her, was minded to put her away privately." Nazareth was a small town, everybody would have known about Mary's condition. But Joseph's unwillingness to expose her to shame suggests that the townspeople saw no sin; they assumed the the child within her was the child of Joseph, her husband.

While he was pondering, "the angel of the Lord appeared to him in sleep". Observe the angel's opening words: "Joseph, son of David, do not be afraid to take thy wife Mary to thyself, for it is by the power of the Holy Ghost that she has conceived this child". So Joseph had been afraid! Now he learns something far greater than the great thing which had happened to Elizabeth—Mary had conceived a child virginally. And he, Joseph, *was* included in God's design for her. By God's command he was to take his virgin wife into his own house.

The angel goes on: "Thou shalt call his name Jesus, for he shall save his people from their sins".

The first six words had already been said to Mary. There was a special significance in their being said to Joseph, whom the angel had saluted as "Joseph, son of David". For Joseph to name the child meant that Joseph accepted him. We speak of Joseph as our Lord's "foster-father". But this is to misunderstand the family law of the Jews. For them, a man who adopted a child *was* the child's father, the word "beget" is actually used of fathers adopting sons. Acceptance by the father was decisive. The accepted son legally acquired not only a father, but all the father's ancestors. For the Jew, Jesus was the son of David because he had been accepted as a son by Joseph, the son of David.

Matthew goes on to make his own comment—that all this was in fulfilment of the prophecy made by Isaiah seven hundred years before: "A virgin shall be with child and bring forth a son; and they shall call his name Emmanuel" (Isaiah 7:14). The word "virgin" is only in the Septuagint translation, the Hebrew word seems to mean "a young unmarried woman". No Jewish commentator had ever seen these words of Isaiah as meaning that the Messiah was to be born of a virgin mother. It is Matthew, inspired by the Holy Ghost, who tells us that they do. And we can know, as the Jews before Christ could not, how marvellously apt was the statement "They shall call his name Emmanuel". The word means "God with us". In fact, it never had been given as a name to any Jew, nor was it now given as a name to Mary's child. But it was a precise statement about what Christ was and is. We compare it, not with the angel's words to Mary and to Joseph: "Thou shalt call his name Jesus", but with Gabriel's words to Mary that he "shall be called the Son of God".

"And Joseph rising up from sleep did as the angel of the Lord commanded him and took unto him his wife." In the tantalizing way of the Evangelists Matthew gives us the essentials, leaving untold so many things we are longing to know—but are forced to admit that we do not strictly need to know! As we have seen, he compresses into forty words Joseph's discovery that Mary was about to bear a child and his reaction to the discovery. Now he needs only half as many to tell us that after the angel's visit Joseph completed the marriage by taking Mary into his own house. And, growing ever terser, he goes on to tell of the birth and naming of the child in some fifteen words.

I have spoken of things untold which we should long to hear. Above all perhaps we wonder about the first meeting with Mary after the angel's message to Joseph. At last she could break her own silence, and tell him what Gabriel had said to her; and Joseph at last could know what the child was whom he was to make legally his own.

Wedding in Nazareth

But we cannot help feeling that Matthew—or at least Luke, who was a shade less reticent—might have told us about the wedding celebrations. We have to be content with what we know of the general pattern of weddings among the Jews. By betrothal, we remember, the couple were made husband and wife. It was the simplest of ceremonies, needing only the presence of two witnesses. The celebrations surrounding the homecoming—that is what the wedding was —were a very different matter, involving every relative and friend that either of them had.

The great day began with the bridegroom and his friends going in procession, with lights and music, to bring the bride from her house to his. Jesus is referring to this procession in the parable about the five silly girls who had no oil for their lamps (Matthew 25). But what exactly was Mary's house? St Luke says that she returned from Judea "to her own house". She must have been living with someone. Luke does not tell us who this someone might be: nor does Matthew—he indeed does not even say that either the angel's visit to Joseph or the marriage took place in Nazareth: the first place he names is Bethlehem, where Christ was born; Nazareth he does not mention till the return from Egypt.

At the bridegroom's house there would be feasting, more or less luxurious according to his wealth or poverty. With the rich, the feast sometimes lasted for days. In the parable of the guest who had no wedding garment (Matthew 22) Our Lord refers to a feast of rather special magnificence—there had been a great slaying of "beeves and fatlings". But that feast was given by a king. The one given by Joseph the carpenter would not have been on that scale. It would probably have been closer to the one given thirty years later in Cana in Galilee (John 2): for that was given by friends of Our Lady, and Cana was only a few miles from Nazareth. There, we may be sure, the beeves and fatlings were in no rich profusion, for the poor of Galilee hardly ever had meat on their tables; we read that the wine ran out; and we may feel reasonably sure that the group of fishermen Jesus brought with him probably wore nothing very special in the way of wedding garments.

How far the wedding feast of Mary and Joseph resembled that of Cana, we can only guess—we simply cannot see either Mary or Joseph putting on any very spectacular show. But one thing the two feasts have in common—Christ was present at both of them! No royal wedding had ever had a glory to compare with that. The poorest Catholic can have it now with a nuptial Mass.

The Voice from the Cross

The Gospels record seven things our Lord said in the three hours he hung on the cross—three of them about others, four about himself. In every one of them we must hear the Priest speaking.

The first—it was spoken before the soldiers proceeded to divide his clothing among themselves—was clearly redemptive: "Father, forgive them, for they know not what they do". He was dying to win forgiveness for the sinful race of man, and his first word of forgiveness concerned his slayers, all of them. Peter (Acts 3:17) makes the same excuse for them—"Brethren, I know that you, like your rulers, acted in ignorance"—Peter did not forget that he himself had had less excuse of ignorance for denying Christ than they for crucifying.

Another thing that Christ said was redemptive, too. When one of the bandits reviled him, the other made the most astounding of all death-bed repentances—if we consider the bed on which he was dying, and the condition of the One in whom he made

c   65 his act of faith. What he said to the man nailed to the next cross was: "Lord, remember me when you come into your kingdom." And Jesus answered his prayer: "*This day* you will be with me in paradise".

The third thing he said about others, which does not appear instantly to have to do with redemption yet most profoundly has. To his mother who was standing before the cross with St John, he said: "Woman, behold your son." And to St John: "Behold you mother". On the surface it is a purely personal, purely domestic remark. But the surface meaning will not do. If he had merely wanted to arrange for someone to look after his mother once he had left the world, he had had plenty of time to do it in the months before. It was not a sudden idea, come to interrupt the offering of his redemptive sacrifice. If he chose to say it at this moment, it was because it belonged to the redemptive process.

The Church sees it as more than the provision of a home for his mother. Mary was being given as Mother not only to John but to all the children of Eve. The Redemption Christ was winning for the race as a whole must be applied to each man individually. In the application, Mary was to play an essential part.

3. Scripture in the Church

"The Church has always venerated the divine Scriptures just as it venerates the body of the Lord, since from the table both of the word of God and of the body of Christ it unceasingly receives and offers to the faithful the bread of life. It has always regarded the Scriptures together with sacred Tradition as the supreme rule of faith, and will ever do so."— *Dogmatic Constitution on Divine Revelation*, VI, 21.

Guidance in Reading Scripture We Must *Have*

Scripture has been given by God to the Church, and by the Church to us. What would it be like without the Church?

The one thing certain is that we could not read it effectively without aid from someone, a great deal of aid. It was written roughly from 900 B.C. to A.D. 100. There are over seventy individual books, so that in one sense it is a library. But more profoundly it is a single book, one part of it throwing light upon another, so that only in the whole book do we get the wholeness of what God is telling us in it. Yet none of the writers, save John, perhaps, could have read the whole book. That at least we can do. But not unaided. And, even with aid, not easily. In the Bible as a whole there is no evident system. At first it seems more like a jungle than a garden, more for exploration than instant delight. And now shall we explore?

As we have noted, there is the question of the religious knowledge, outlook, practices which the writer is taking for granted in his readers. It is difficult enough for us to know with certainty either what these were in themselves or what they meant in the living fact, even for the half century within which the New Testament was written. It is more difficult still for the centuries that came and went as the Old Testament books grew to their present form, and quite immeasurably difficult for the ages into which they reach back.

Then there is the history of all that thousand-year period: the writers assume knowledge of events now forgotten, situation long vanished. Consider the Gospel only. The trial and death of our Lord are almost incomprehensible if we do not know how the Romans came to be ruling Palestine, what Herod's position was, what rights the religious leaders of the Jews had.

His relations with his own people are wholly incomprehensible if we do not know that the Sadducees were the dominant party and stood for collaboration with Rome, if we attach no idea to the Pharisees save hypocrisy; if we do not know all the complex of ideas bound up with "the multitude", what the Jewish expectation of the Messiah was *at that time*, what the Jewish feasts signify, what a synagogue service was, what the phrase "Son of Man" suggested to those who heard it. Without all this knowledge the reader can get an impressionistic sketch of a good man misunderstood and maltreated, but he cannot pretend to know what is really happening.

There is a difficulty of another sort than the historical knowledge which the Bible assumes and does not provide. We, differently formed, are reading a book written by Semites for Semites. We have to be told just about everything. Of ourselves we should not know that the tremendous words of the prophet Joel, used of Christ's death by Peter in his first Pentecost speech, about the moon being turned into blood and stars falling out of the sky—were quite normally used, right into the Middle Ages, about the death of any outstanding Jew: they were not astronomical at all. When, as we have already noted, the writer of the Book of Wisdom talks as if he were the centuries-dead King Solomon, he was not being guilty of a forgery, he was using a literary device conventional in his world. And for many a century men read the Book of Jonah without any suspicion that it might be a kind of extended parable, directed against racial arrogance.

There is the question of the languages in which the books were written, the meaning of the words. We find ourselves watching, lost but fascinated, the battle between the philologists who specialize in language and the exegetes whose concern is with the message. For words are only a part of the problem. What was in the mind of the author, what was he setting out to do or show? What did he regard as primary? What did he affirm, what did he simply take in his stride? Where is he using a document that has come his way? There are, as we have seen, prophecies unfulfilled. And the prophets themselves show great changes of outlook and teaching—the collapse of all that David and Solomon had built, followed by the forty years of the Babylonian Captivity, made an immense difference to them. How is the ordinary reader to evaluate all this or even know it?

The whole thing is too vast. The details are myriad, but even to know them all—which even the greatest scholar could not possibly do—would not be enough. Prophecy must be taken massively. Yet the totality of prophecy is harder for us to make our own than the myriad details. It is not too much to say that Israel itself was a prophetical fact— prophecy incarnate in this one people—as Christ was the Word, incarnate in this one man: Christ was the Word which prophecy existed to utter.

Without guidance we are first confused, then discouraged. Even those who persevere do not get a tithe of what is there to be got. One can, of course, read Scripture in a state of pious coma, feeling that the general experience is uplifting and not expecting any very specific meaning—rather like listening to a lovely voice singing in a language we do not know. But this is fooling oneself. To read the Bible without external aids is to fail to take it seriously. "The word of God is living and effectual and more piercing than any two-edged sword": is Scripture so to us? A two-edged sword is not meant for playing with. Aid in using Scripture we must indeed have: the Bible read without commentary is like a landscape before sunrise; it is all there of course, but not to the eye: and if one does not accept the Church, there are only the scholars.

Do not let the word "only" suggest that the

scholars are not doing a mighty, and mightily valuable, work. Their work on the texts we should know to be essential, even if *Divino Afflante* had not told us so. Their work on the languages, and on the shifts of meaning of individual words from one age to another, has made passage after passage of Scripture a new thing. And linguistics is not the whole, or even the main, of it. Their discoveries of similarity, of religious episodes and ideas, to be found in the religions of paganism before we find them in Scripture is the most moving reminder that God did not leave men at any time without his help, unless they themselves refused it. We have noted that the Egyptians honoured the Sun with a hymn which could become Psalm 104, and that a great part of Psalm 28 had been chanted for Baal. There was a great flame of prayer going up from men to God all over the world, and God has his own ways of responding, appropriate to their powers of acceptance.

But we must approach the scholars with care all the same, in the religious field especially, but not only in that. It is possible to know every word in the dictionary and even be able to add one's own supplement to the dictionary, and yet be unable to write a living sentence oneself, or even to respond to the life in the writing of other men. A given scholar might study Shakespeare, for instance—vocabulary, grammar, scansion, sources, the age in which he lived, and every first-rate critic who has ever written on him—and simply not "get" Shakespeare at all.

73

It is for us to learn what the learned have to teach us, and then read Shakespeare. We lend them our ears, but not our mind. We bring to our reading the self that we are. Shakespeare must find us responsive. So must God.

There are of course great commentators, whom we are the richer for reading. Yet even the greatest cannot do otherwise than bring to the reading and interpretation his own philosophy of life, the experience life has brought him as he has lived it. And that means that he brings not only strengths but limitations, his own limitations and those of his age. Today's scholars see the weaknesses of yesterday's, but only the greatest of them see that today will soon be yesterday. They feel that they have transcended earlier thinkers, but only the rare ones see themselves as transcendable in their turn. Only the exceptional teacher takes absolutely for granted that his best pupils will outgrow him—indeed that his function is to help them to. But if the scholars seem to forget it, we who read them must not.

And there is something else. The man who does not believe in God *must* read Scripture differently from the man who does. Or again the man who accepts God's existence but whose every instinct shrinks away from God's intervention in human affairs, reads Scripture differently from one whose mind is open on the matter. For all practical purposes the man who believes that Christ is God and the man who does not are reading two different books: a discussion between them as to the meaning of the

74

New Testament is as though one were discussing marriage with a eunuch.

When Peter's Second Epistle (1:20) says, "No prophecy of Scripture is a matter of one's own interpretation", it is saying that one needs aid from the teaching of the Church, not from the consensus of scholarship. But without the Church, men are at the mercy of scholars, who have so little mercy on one another.

Doctrine and Scripture Not Simply Different Arrangements of the Same Material

There is endless conflict, and no referee. And in the nature of the case there can be no merely human referee. Revelation is a matter not only of light seen, but of a seeing mind enriched in its very substance. "May the Father grant you a spirit of wisdom and insight, to give you a fuller knowledge of himself. May your inward eye be enlightened" (Ephesians 1:18). While the conflict goes on, men are unnourished, left in darkness.

That may be regarded as St Paul's commentary on the words of our Lord: "Anyone who is prepared to do his will shall know of the doctrine, whether it be of God or whether I speak of myself" (John 7:17). Our Lord is not saying that teaching is unnecessary if one does God's will, but that the doing of God's will is an essential precondition for the understanding of God's word. And this not solely because obedience deserves so great a reward, but that doing

God's will is nourishing, muscle-building, health-giving, an enriching of the self to whom God's word is addressed. Yves Congar speaks of "the fundamental error of believing that by an exegetico-historical study it can be decided what Christians should hold". And his fellow Dominican, Pierre Benoit, writes: "How are we to know that we have not substituted the exegesis of our spirit for the exegesis of God's spirit? Only a public authority divinely guided can spell out without error a public message divinely revealed".

Masses and masses of the truth God wants us to know here on earth can be drawn out of the Scriptures, but not necessarily by the individual reader, or by any number of individual readers. The Word in his Body not only bears witness to Himself in Scripture, but watches over the teaching, the interpretation, the application, the whole immense process of unfolding.

Even one who believes none of this does see that there has been an unfolding. The Jews have had one —within the Old Testament itself and subsequent to it, Mishna developing Torah, Talmud developing Mishna. To quote Père Benoit again: "The very words of the inspired ancients have received, in the vast perspective of the divine plan, a richness and fullness that their first authors have not conceived, but by which future readers were to profit—e.g., those who centuries later could compare one with another the messianic prophecies of an Isaiah, a Jeremiah, a Daniel, and could compare them with their fulfilment in Christ had a more lucid and deeper understanding than those to whom they were first revealed. Or again, the knowledge of the mystery of the Trinity enables us to read with a new eye the words of the Old Testament on Wisdom. Thus God has commented His own word by itself, illuminated the old utterances by new, giving them a wider reach, which one calls the *sensus plenior*".

Our Lord fills the Old Testament themes of King, Son of Man, Servant, Redeemer, with a content of which the Old Testament gives only glimpses. To read the Old Testament without knowing the New means to miss this rich content. Similarly if we know the New Testament without knowing the Church's long meditation on it, its long labour on it, in the power of the Word whose Body the Church is, then equally we are missing richness that God means for us. There is so much that the Old Testament writers had not. It is all in the New Testament, of course— but rather as the whole truth of God is in the phrase of Deuteronomy "I Am": it is all there, but we cannot unpack it. To dismiss what the Church, living in Christ and in-lived by the Holy Spirit, has made of it in near two thousand years, is to impoverish ourselves.

Not that the Church comments on Scripture, verse by verse. There are, indeed, only a handful of verses to which it has attached an authoritative interpretation. It is there to teach of God and of man's way to God *in the very fullness of our present knowledge*. The Church's subject matter, in fact, is Reality as it exists. But in this teaching it is continually nourished, and nourishes us, upon Scripture and Sacrament—we may feel that to be nourished by the Eucharist without the Scripture is better than to try to nourish oneself by Scripture without the Eucharist, but either course would be a putting asunder of two that God has joined. The same Holy Ghost by whom the Word of God was conceived in the body of Mary caused the Word of God to be conceived in the minds of the writers of Scripture. Thus nourished and living in the truth, the Church sees and tells us more of Reality, and thereby casts further light upon the Scripture from which it has already drawn so much light.

The doctrine it teaches does not necessarily decide what given passages of Scripture mean. Doctrine and Scripture are not simply different arrangements of the same material. *They are two approaches from different angles to one same Reality.* There are elements in Scripture which the teaching Church has not yet crystallized in doctrine, and there are elements in the doctrine which are not explicit in Scripture. Each sheds light, but the two may not always combine—for us—in one single luminous stream, any more than the elements in a given dogma do. We may twist the meaning of texts in an effort to force them to support a particular doctrine; but it will be rather like the oddity called Concordism round the turn of the century, the effort to make Genesis say what the newest scientists were saying about Creation and Evolution. On the relation between Scripture and the Church's teaching,

Newman stated the principle: "The question", says Newman, "is not whether this or that proposition of Catholic doctrine is *in terminis* in Scripture, unless we would be slaves to the letter, but whether that one view of the mystery, of which all such are exponents, be not there".

The Unfolding of Revelation

This unfolding of the truths contained in the Deposit of Faith is carried out by scholars, by the men who have to conduct the daily running of the Church, by the mass of ordinary people living by the truths. There are the Fathers and Doctors, not possessed of all the knowledge that the modern savant has, but saints every one of them, and as such entitled to that insight which Christ has promised to those who do God's will. There are whole armies of theologians and Scripture scholars. What emerges from all this work may find universal acceptance, so that it may fairly be said that the Church teaches it: some of this universally accepted doctrine reaches definition by Pope or Council. But there are always elements which are accepted in one place or another, so that to masses of Catholics they seem plain matters of faith, yet time winnows them.

But we shall not understand the whole process of unfolding if we think of it as simply a means of drawing the *logical* consequences from the elements first committed to the Apostles. That is one way, but not the only way. There is another way, which we may call *organic:* This really *is* impact. Christians, living in and by the truths, living them in Christ, come to the certainty that other things must be true too, although the connection could not be stated mathematically. An example is the clearer light in which Christ's Mother came to be seen, as men grew into, and grew in, the explication of the reality of Christ himself. Living in the truth that Mary had conceived a son who was God, and in those other truths concerning sanctifying grace and God's plan for the restoration of the fullness of manhood by the resurrection of the body at the end of time, men grew to see it as unthinkable that she should ever have existed without sanctifying grace or that she should not now be present with her Son in the fullness of her humanity: this sort of certainty does not perhaps exclude all possibility of error, though the possibility dwindles to vanishing point when the new truth is held by all over a very long space of time. In these two instances, the Church settled the matter with the defined dogmas of the Immaculate Conception and the Assumption.

The Old Testament writers had not heard the truths that Christ was to reveal, had not received Christ sacramentally; they had been in-lived by the Holy Spirit indeed, but not as he in-lived Christ. And quite apart from the supernatural realities, they had not had the widening of natural mental outlook which would have come from long-continued mental and spiritual contact with cultures very different from their own. The Jews are a remarkable people, but they do not exhaust either the mental or the spiritual resources of the human race. Already in the Old Testament we can see something of what they drew from Babylonian and Persian culture; as well as a bare beginning of what the Church was to gain in enrichment from the Greeks. There are other cultures still—Hindu and Chinese, for example—and who knows what still remains for them to give us, who knows what development of our understanding of Revelation there would have been if the Church had moved Eastward instead of Westward? Or indeed if the Word had been made flesh in Asia, not in Asia Minor. . . .

But in the providence of God it was the Greek enrichment that the study of Revelation has most notably had. And the Old Testament writers did not have it. We must not canonize their limitations or be congealed in them. To repeat a point already made about one of these limitations—they thought that God could be known only in his actions and not in his innermost self. They would have listened uncomprehending to St Paul's clear statement that man's mind can see even the depths of God (1 Corinthians 13:2; 10:16), just as they did listen uncomprehending to the words of our Lord upon which Paul is here making his own comment—"No one knows the Father but the Son, and him to whom the Son shall reveal him" (Matthew 11:27).

The New Testament writers did not share this first limitation of their predecessors, for they had

81

the revelation of Christ. Yet certain things, and these immensely educative, they had not had. They had not had seventy generations of living in and by the truths Christ revealed and of receiving the life that comes from him. They had not seen the truths challenged by new situations—one wonders, indeed, if any writer of either Testament had ever had an argument with an atheist. And there are all sorts of other experiences they had not had, experiences which would have taken them deeper into the revelation they had received. St Peter had not met, or possibly dreamed of, some of his successors in the Papacy—John XII for instance; St Paul had not seen the Inquisition—he lists his own sufferings in no awareness that some of his successors would inflict these same sufferings on others. Our Lord learnt obedience by the things he suffered (Hebrews 5:8): his Church has learnt a great deal by the things it in its turn has suffered, and something perhaps from the sufferings it has caused other men to undergo.

One way or another there has been a continual growth of realization of the truths Christ entrusted to men. The Deposit of Faith was not a talent to be buried in the ground or wrapped in a napkin for fear of contamination. It is closer to reality to think of it as a seed—and in no seed is all the fruit that is to grow from it plainly contained.

Infallibility, guaranteed by Christ to his Church, is a reality, just as the inspiration of Scripture is a reality. Uncertainty as to what Scripture means—

that is as to what the words meant to the man who wrote them—does not keep us in uncertainty as to what God has revealed, if the Church has defined it. Our deepest concern must always be not with as much of the truth as the original writer saw, but with what God can bring to light *in us* upon the reality of himself, and ourselves, and our way to him.

But if one does not see the Church as the Mystical Body in which the Word is continuously in operation, this channel of light is not known to be available— above all, when there is question of a development of what I have called the organic kind as distinct from the purely logical. We saw this very clearly after the definition of the dogma of the Assumption of our Lady into heaven. Those men did not fall behind us in devotion to Scripture who at that time said that their Church "refuses to regard as requisite for saving faith any doctrine or opinions not plainly contained in the Scriptures".

Three comments suggest themselves. (1) Fruit is no less from seed because not plainly contained in it: unless you are a botanist you might look long at a seed with no notion of what fruit was meant to come from it; even a botanist cannot know all of what soil and sun might do to it: and this seed was unique like none that botany knew. (2) A thing may be quite plain, yet not to us—because of a defect in our vision; and there are areas of obscurity which can grow luminous as the Holy Spirit gives increase of light. (3) Leaving the Church out of it, but considering only what the scholars have had to say, one

83

wonders how many texts of Scripture are left with a meaning so plain that all sane readers must accept it.

Let us look longer at the phrase "requisite for saving faith". Actually the question whether a given truth or practice is necessary for salvation cannot possibly be the primary test. God being merciful, we can be saved on such a bare minimum of knowledge of what he has revealed. But even if great numbers of truths were necessary to be known if we are to be saved, that would not be the principal reason for knowing them. To hold that it is would make ourselves central instead of seeing God as central. Truth is still worth having because it is true, even if we could be saved without knowing it.

And what about the necessity of truth for love? Each new thing learnt about God is a new reason for loving him. Can we imagine anyone saying, provided he was really listening to what he was saying: "We don't need to know any more about God or his work, we know enough already for our salvation"? Love of God, as of our fellow men, craves knowledge and is fed by it.

The Two Testaments Need Each Other but Not Equally

Christopher Dawson has said that a society which does not know its own history is like a man suffering from amnesia. We cannot really know where we are, if we do not know how we got here. This applies to the Christian community. As we have already noted, one value of following the story of Redemption in the Old Testament is simply that men passed that way, and that we should not be where we are now if they had not.

This does not mean that we should begin our study of Revelation with the Old Testament and work forward: that would be rather like beginning the study of astronomy with—say—the Chaldeans, passing on to Ptolemy, on to Galileo, making a detour to study the Mayans, arriving at last at the structure and operation of the heavens as we now know them to be. A ship should be steered by all relevant knowledge now available, so should man's life. To begin with the most primitive and work forward would be a strange way of study in any field. In the redemptive field it would involve us in two difficulties special to itself.

The first of these is that most of what is called salvation history is in fact *not* history as modern scholars have conditioned us to understand the word. It is true, but in its own order. Adam, for instance: we do not know what his name was—Adam means "man"—or where he lived, or what language he spoke, or (within half-a-million years or so) when he lived; the account of him in Genesis was written a few hundred years before Christ, we do not know by whom, or what authority he had. With Noah as second ancestor of the whole race, with the flood, the Ark and the animals, even conservative believers will hardly assert that we are in touch with history in the modern sense. As Ronald Knox writes:

First Adam fell, then Noah's ark was drowned,
And Samson under close inspection bound.
For Daniel's blood the critic lions roared
And trembling hands threw Jonah overboard.

Samson and Daniel and Jonah matter less. But how much do we know of those key figures, Abraham and Moses? What are the credentials *as history* of Deuteronomy?

It is becoming clear that there is more sheer history in the Old Testament than men thought round the turn of the century, but only one trained in the relevant highly specialized disciplines can evaluate the arguments for the historicity of any given statement. Any text can prove to be a battle-ground, and the battle is not for beginners.

I imagine scholars, hearing the phrase "salvation history", might ask, "Don't you mean salvation midrash?" "Midrash" is a Hebrew word used of episodes or teachings valuable for their spiritual meaning but not meant as statements of historical fact: our Lord's parables are examples.

But with the word "meaning" we come to that other profounder reason for not beginning our study of Revelation with Salvation History. It is that the true beginning is Christ: "No one comes to the Father but by me". That other word of his, "I am the door", has a wider application than entry into the Church here and now. It means entry into the

whole Christian inheritance—including the fulfilment in which the Old Testament receives its
meaning. To one who did not know the New
Testament, the line of Salvation History we trace
would seem highly artificial, just too selective.

For the understanding of the Old Testament we
need the New, for the understanding of the New we
need the Old Testament. But the two "needs" are
not equal. The New Testament is fulfilment,
luminous in itself but yielding more light still if we
know what came before. Whereas without knowledge of the fulfilment, the Old Testament has too
much of its light locked up within it. One might find
it a maze rather than a road. As we noted earlier, to
one who came to it unprepared, it would be more like
a jungle he was not equipped to explore than a
garden for present pleasure. Pleasure? Only the
toughest manage to read it from beginning to end—a
fact of some pedagogical bearing. In all honesty
most of us admit weariness to the heart in great
tracts of it, and revolt in the heart at some of it.

Though the New Testament writers revel in the
Old Testament prefigurings, we do not find them
urging those first Christians to read it. Timothy is
approved of (2 Timothy 3:15) for having read it,
and it is worth noticing the terms in which its value
is expressed—"*profitable* for teaching, for reproof,
for correction and for training in righteousness, that
the man of God may be *complete, equipped for every
good work*". The *Constitution on Divine Revelation*
says: "The books of the Old Testament, even

87

though they contain much that is temporary and provisional, are *of importance* even to Christ's faithful in setting down the divine teaching."

"Profitable," "of importance." To Old Testament lovers the words sound a shade measured, they would have liked something stronger, closer to the vehemence of the phrase about Scripture as a whole in the Encyclical *Humani Generis*, "Without Biblical theology dogmatic theology becomes *sterile*". Certainly for the serious student of theology the Old Testament is essential.

It may be helpful to summarize certain principles here.

(1) The weariness of spirit and the horror may never, for some of us, wholly cease; but they will not be dominant. We shall find a growing excitement as we recognize the first shadowings of realities we have met in the New Testament—the kind of phrases or happenings which cause the New Testament writers to attach to so much of what they are recording the words "that the Scripture might be fulfilled". These may be vast things like Passover and Pasch, or simply verbal felicities—like discovering that a couple of words in Luke's first chapter had already been used—and so fittingly—in the Greek version of the Old Testament. The same Greek verb is used in Exodus for the cloud that *abode* upon the meeting-tent of Moses when the glory of the Lord filled the tabernacle, and for the power of the Most High *overshadowing* Mary of Nazareth when the

Lord entered her womb. Similarly the Greek verb used (2 Samuel 6:14–16) for David *dancing* before the Ark (which contained the written word of God) is used again for John the Baptist *leaping* in his Mother's womb when Mary entered Elizabeth's house.

The Old Testament is full of such excitements, smaller and greater. We must indeed be on our guard against a danger which sounds improbable but continues to take its toll. It is possible to develop an unbalanced interest in the prefigurings, to the point where we can see no value in the fulfilment till we have found something in the Old Testament which we can feel that it fulfils.

Paul warned the Colossians (2:16) about due proportion—"These are only a shadow of what is to come, but the substance belongs to Christ". As Shakespeare said in another context, "The best in this sort are but shadows". The primary importance is in the thing Christ did or suffered or said—there is always more in that than in its prefiguring. Christ brought us salvation, but we hear no word from him of Adam's sin which lies at the beginning of the road that leads to himself. Paul shows us Adam as a type of Christ, but we hear no suggestion of this from Christ's lips.

The Old Testament has a power to fascinate—I have known Catholic scholars so much in the grip of its fascination that the whole New Testament seems to them only a postscript to it. There are commentators who to all appearance find nothing

89

worthy of attention in the New Testament save texts from the Old misunderstood by the writers of the New who lacked the equipment of modern scholarship!

They did lack it, of course, but they had a different approach as well. In any given thing they could see the whole story of Redemption, and often enough that is all they are saying with the phrase "that the Scriptures might be fulfilled". When Matthew spoke of the return of the Holy Family after the flight from Herod as a fulfilment of the text of Hosea "Out of Egypt I called my son," he knew of course that Hosea was talking of Israel's Exodus from Egypt. But the mere aptness of the words to the present situation delighted him, especially perhaps because of the words preceding those he quoted—"When Israel was a child I loved him".

(2) If we accept Scripture and the Church as two ways of the Word's utterance we do not force either to say what the other is saying on any given point, we simply do our best to find what each *is* saying; but we do reject any interpretation of either which would make it contradict the other. The Church cannot contradict Scripture, Scripture cannot contradict the Church.

Both these statements are true, but one is easier to apply than the other. We can see at once if an interpretation of Scripture is irreconcilable with Catholic doctrine. Those who see Christ's words "Why do you call me good, none is good but God?"

as an assertion that he is not God, are plainly denying the doctrine of the Incarnation. Those who see his words "He that believes and is baptized shall be saved" as forbidding the baptism of infants are plainly denying the doctrine that the grace given in baptism is for all.

But those who feel that a given Catholic doctrine is irreconcilable with Scripture have to face the difficulty we have already noted—that more than one interpretation is possible for practically any text that is not a simple statement of simple fact. Thus, I imagine, Catholics have always taken for granted that Simeon's words in the temple, "Thine own soul a sword shall pierce" (Luke 1:35), refer to what Christ's Mother is to suffer. But Père Benoit argues that they are not about her at all, but about Christians generally, very much as Christ's words from the Cross "Behold thy mother" gave Mary as Mother not to John only but to Christians generally: and that the "sword" does not mean suffering but is "the word of God, sharper than any two-edged sword, piercing to the division of soul and spirit . . . and discerning the thoughts and intentions of the heart" (Hebrews 4:12). This is one text out of thousands, where any one interpretation may be challenged by some other.

The Church's teaching, being formalized and organized, is less subject to a variety of interpretations. And when it is, we can ask the Church to clarify as we cannot ask the Bible. The answer to the question with which I began this chapter is in two sentences: Without the Church what I could do to the Bible! But with the Church what the Bible does to me.

The possibility that they can be asked for a fuller explanation must always be a difference between the living teachers actually present and the books written by men long in heaven. The difference is more strongly marked today. As Karl Rahner has noted in *Nature and Grace:* "It has never been so easy to know clearly what Christ teaches as it is in this, our modern age, when the Church (above all since the First Vatican Council) has developed its understanding of itself to the point of formulating precisely and finally the nature of its teaching authority and the way in which it functions". The Second Vatican Council has shown that there are still problems to be examined; but, as to the mass of the Church's teaching, there are not so much problems, as the invitation to thrust deeper, to widen the area on which the light falls.

Reading Scripture for Vital Equivalents

The Old Testament tells the story of the preparation but it is not a blueprint, not history written in advance. If you had only the Old Testament, you could not possibly see in advance what the fulfilment would be. But study what Christ in fact was and in fact did, then re-read the Old Testament and you will find it incredibly fulfilled, fulfilled beyond all measure and all possibility of foreseeing, but fulfilled all the same, and unmistakably. We have just glanced at 2 Timothy 3:16—about the profitableness of the Old Testament. But we may not remember the verse immediately before: "From your infancy you have known the Holy Scriptures, which can instruct you to salvation, *by the faith which is in Christ Jesus*".

To have lived generation after generation in Christ and in the light of his revelation makes a difference beyond all measuring. Yet we can still go back to the New Testament writers who had had the experience of Christ only so newly and so recently, and to the Old Testament writers who had not had the experience at all. Why?

There is a way of return to Scripture which is a kind of self-indulgence. The plain truth is that there is a burden in the thought-structure which, under the guidance of the Holy Spirit, his Church has erected in nineteen hundred years. To bury oneself in the inspired books can simply be a way of unshouldering the burden. If we select carefully, there are lovely words and deeds in Scripture which set the emotions vibrating without calling upon the mind for labour and sweat, and in these vibrations we can luxuriate. And indeed we should: there is health in occasional luxury.

But that must never be our sole way of return. There are profounder reasons. For in the first place God is in them as in no other writing. They are a permanent presence of God communicating and energizing.

93

Every reader must have had the experience of coming upon phrases which say something special to himself, as if they had been written for him alone. The Holy Spirit abides in the inspired writing and our souls can still make contact with him: nor is there anything written since in which we have so present a consciousness of God's majesty and our own nothingness. It aids in *our* concrete situation to see what a particular Prophet made of *his:* with all that we have and he had not of revelation and sacrament, his intensity does something for our pallor.

We shall be reading for vital equivalents as well as mental. Thus we might very well learn the whole doctrine on the Virgin Mother of Christ as the Church gives it to us, then re-read all that is relevant to her in the New Testament. If then we go to the Old Testament and concentrate not only upon her as we find gleams and glimpses of her there, but also upon the rich thread of teaching on the Virgin Israel, then, however much or little the original writer saw, what he has written operates in us most powerfully not for illumination only, but for vitalization.

And so with every element in the Revelation—Scripture enriches, gives life, widens the horizon. So St Paul told the Romans (15:4): "What things soever were written, were written for our learning: that through patience and the comfort of the Scriptures, we might have hope".

Remember that for St Paul hope and vitality are

inseparable. And remember, too, that "comfort" has not our modern meaning: it means strengthening. To cope with some of what we shall meet in the Old Testament, that strengthening will be needed.

4. Mass and Eucharist

"The liturgy is made up of unchangeable elements divinely instituted, and elements subject to change. The latter not only may but ought to be changed with the passing of time if features have by chance crept in which are less harmonious with the intimate nature of the liturgy, or if existing elements have grown less functional. In this restoration, both texts and rites should be drawn up so that they express more clearly the holy things which they signify. Christian people, as far as possible, should be able to understand them with ease and to take part in them fully, actively, and as and as befits a community."—*Constitution on the Sacred Liturgy*, III, 21.

I

For the man-in-the-pew the question, "Is it the same Church?" often enough boils down to the question, "Is it the same Mass?" The changes there are so obvious—the high altar practically ignored and the tabernacle hard to find; the priest facing the people when he isn't sitting with folded hands, while members of the congregation read aloud; fasting before Communion reduced almost out of existence; Latin yielding place to English, all expected to dialogue, and to sing as they go to Communion; no last Gospel; octaves banished from Epiphany, Ascension, Corpus Christi. If he reads the papers he finds startling things said and startling things suggested—about the Real Presence, our Lady's virginity, what you will. There is hardly a doctrine or practice of the Church one has not heard attacked. He finds it all very confusing, rather disturbing, but not very real, in the nature of the stage direction "Noises off".

But the Mass is close to him. If only they would leave the Mass alone, he feels, he could go on practising his Faith till it all blows over. He had loved the Mass; he knew where he was in it. And now they have changed it without a word of consultation with him or his sort. He wouldn't have made a grievance of that, for the Church has no habit of consulting the laity, if they hadn't just been telling him of the laity's priesthood—and the Mass is the priestliest action of all.

For myself, I found it hard to get used to the new way. It was after some weeks of the changed ritual that I answered the priest's words "The Body of Christ" with "Thank you" (but then ritual isn't my strong point—I once poured wine instead of water over the priest's fingers at the Lavabo). But I like most of the changes (I don't like the hymn-singing, especially when I am at the altar rail; I am not given to singing at meals). But there are still many who dislike the "new" Mass bitterly.

It is partly a matter of emotional attachment to something one has always had. Changing it feels like an uprooting. There was a time in the Eastern Church when men were slaying one another over the question whether the priest's blessing should be given with one finger upraised or two. I have met people really uneasy at the Pope's abolition of the Lenten fast—one remembers the reaction of the Irish in the last century when Pope Leo XIII, who had just condemned an effort by the tenants to win justice from the landlords, dispensed them from abstinence because of an influenza epidemic. Better for him, they said, if he left politics alone and minded his religion.

Things we have grown used to come to seem of the

essence. It does us good to re-examine them, and learn what is or is not essential. We are hearing it said that, in this matter of changes in the Mass, the Church is admitting that Luther was right after all. But—as Luther knew—the use of the vernacular instead of Latin is a detail compared with the doctrine of the Mass as a Sacrifice; receiving the Eucharist in both kinds is a trifle compared with whether, or in what sense, Christ our Lord is really present in either kind, just as whether priests may marry is a trifle compared with the reality of the Apostolic Succession.

It is pretty certain that we are not at the end of changes. Catholics with their eyes fixed on the Last Supper want to be rid of vestments and see Mass restored to the dining room: my wife remembers back fifteen years to the first time she was at a Mass said by a priest-workman at the kitchen table, and very moving she found it. But it was a long way from the ideal of those to whom Mass means Latin murmured in a dark church. And there are those to whom Church music means Gregorian Chant in a Gothic abbey (like the buzzing of bees in a bottle, an irreverent friend of mine said): they may not be enthusiastic about the Missa Luba of African Catholics or the Flamenco-style Mass now being prepared in Spain.

I have mentioned the priest—at a church for which I have a special love—who was so seized with the doctrine of the priesthood of the laity that he would put the Host into the hands of communicants so that they might minister it to themselves. That practice was stopped. But it has returned. After all it happened that way in the earlier centuries.

Who knows indeed? The question "what next?" sets the tone of all present discussion of the Mass. Changes which have happened, changes which may happen, are argued over passionately wherever Catholics meet. The quietest people find themselves shouting. We are back in the fourth century when men would have the cutting of their hair interrupted while the barber argued about the relation of Father and Son in the Trinity.

We are right to see the Liturgy as vitally important. It was no accident that the Second Vatican Council gave itself first to Liturgical Revival and Development. *The Mass is the one place where we meet God, not as individuals (which we can do at any moment) but as his People.* Unless this meeting is right, nothing else in the Church will be.

The Council thought that the Mass matters. So do we of the laity. But we and the Council may not always have been on the same wavelength. When Pope Paul spoke, as he did at a weekly audience, of a devout layman who "was happy because *for the first time in his life* he had participated in the Sacrifice of the Mass to the full spiritual measure", many of us were forced to rethink the Mass. What is this "full spiritual measure" which is made possible by the changes in the ritual? Have we all these years been content with some lesser measure?

The key is perhaps contained in the phrase in which discontent at the changes is often expressed—

"There's no peace". Those to whom Mass was a time for being alone with God feel that the congregation is crowding in on the intimacy of their converse with Him. And in the din of the dialogue they can't hear themselves pray.

In all this there is a profound spirituality, but it may be missing the point of the Mass. "Liturgical services are not private functions", says the Council. We go to Mass *in order* to join with others in an action we and they are performing together. And that action-with-others is not simply praying, as when we say the Rosary together or sing the *Te Deum*. It is the offering to God of Christ once slain on Calvary and now forever living, as Vatican II expressed it (*Constitution on the Church, III*, 28)—"until the coming of the Lord, the one sacrifice of the New Testament—the sacrifice of Christ offering himself once and for all to His Father as a spotless victim—is represented and applied in the Sacrifice of the Mass".

The priest consecrates and offers in the power of Christ; and we are not merely spectators watching or an audience listening, however devotionally. We are partners in the offering: "*my sacrifice and yours*", says the priest to use at the *Orate fratres*. The Council gives our priesthood rich expression. "The faithful join in the offering of the Eucharist by virtue of their royal priesthood" (*Constitution on the Church, II*, 10). "The faithful offer the Immaculate Victim not only through the hands of the priest but also *with him*" (*Constitution on the Liturgy, II*, 48).

Compared with the immensity of what is being

done at Mass, questions of Latin or vernacular, silence or dialogue, are secondary—not unimportant but not primary either. We cannot profitably argue about how the Mass should be said till we have brought our whole mind to bear upon what the Mass is.

What in hard fact is our state of mind, our state of spirit, during Mass? In his poem *Christmas Eve and Easter Day* Robert Browning describes Catholics at Mass:

> All famishing with expectation
> Of the main altar's consummation

Happy you and I if that is our state. But is it? Let us admit that we don't all, or always, look as if we were famishing, or even particularly expectant.

Not that that proves anything. The Host does not look as if Christ were present in it, the communicant often enough does not look as if Christ were present in him. In neither instance does the look tell the whole story. But at least we know that it is hard to maintain realization at full intensity. We have had the experience of the Mass so often that we hardly experience it any more.

Considering the immensity of what Christ is doing, one would think it impossible for the mind to wander for so much as an instant. An instant? Distraction can occupy half our Mass time. I haven't a doubt that men have died for the Mass who suffered distraction at every Mass they ever heard.

Even those who feel nostalgia for the Mass that is

gone can hardly deny that they experience less distraction from what is being done at the altar at the new dialogued Mass in the vernacular. As Pope Paul put it at one of his weekly audiences: "Previously our presence was sufficient; now attention is demanded, and action. Previously one could doze, but no longer".

To be free from distraction because there is constantly something for us to say is at least better than day-dreaming. And the words we now find ourselves saying, and saying aloud, with men on each side of us saying them too, can do strange things to us. But ideally we should be held by what the Mass exists to do: That should become so real to us, so in-built, that *of itself* it grips our whole mind and heart.

We should be livingly conscious of what Mass is, conscious not only of what is being done but of ourselves as taking part in the doing. The Church, says the Council in a stunning phrase, is the sacrament of the salvation of the whole world: and the Mass is a sort of burning-glass focussing that sacrament.

Or rather it focusses Christ. Ask the first dozen Christians you meet—"What is Christ doing now?" Unless one can answer that, one cannot understand the Mass. Over the years I have put the question to crowds in Hyde Park, London, and Times Square, New York. Those who don't care naturally have no answer. But even many who truly love our Lord cannot imagine anything He need do now—after all, He said on the Cross: "It is finished".

It is rare to have anyone quote, "He is living on *to make intercession for us*", still less the word which precede these—"Jesus continues for ever and *his priestly office is unchanging:* that is why he can give eternal salvation to those who through him make their way to God" (Hebrews 7:24–25, Knox). "Christ has entered into heaven itself, now to appear in the presence of God on our behalf" (Hebrews 9:24, RSV).

So that is what he is doing now and always—making intercession for us as priest. How? By "standing as a lamb slain" (Revelation 5:6,12). He appears before God with the marks of his wounding showing, glowing.

His redeeming sacrifice—Death, Resurrection, Ascension—was complete, but it still has to be applied to each individual human being, and it is by this that he applies it.

That is Christ's work "on our behalf" in heaven. Because he wills it so, it breaks through to our altars. The priest in Christ's name, by Christ's power, offers the same Christ—there on the altar in the appearance of bread and wine—to the same Father for the same saving purpose. Christ is doing this at the altar, the priest is doing it with him. And we are doing it too.

How do we of the laity come in? In St Thomas' phrase, Baptism is a sharing in the priesthood of Christ, and so is Confirmation; with Holy Orders priesthood here on earth is completed, but even without that we have some part in Christ the Priest.

By Baptism we are elements in the Body of that Christ who is being offered, in whose power the priest makes the offering, and we with him. We cannot help being part of the action of the Mass. We can only behave as if we were not.

It is strange that we should ever forget this prime fact about our baptized selves. We are nobody in particular but, compared with members of Christ, no one is anybody! It is strangest of all if we forget it at Mass—if we "go to" Mass not seeing our Lord as he is in heaven, offering himself, once slain but now forever living, to his Father; not seeing the priest and ourselves, in the power of what is happening in heaven, offering the same Lord to the same Father. The Mass is Calvary as Christ is now offering it to his heavenly Father. If we do thus *see* Mass, we are in a better position to discuss the changes.

II

When, with the Council in full flow, Pope Paul issued an encyclical on the Blessed Eucharist the ordinary Catholic was puzzled. The Council was deeply involved with quite different questions: what was so urgent about this one? The document itself did nothing to relieve his puzzlement. It was simply the straight doctrine of the Eucharist as he had known it all his Catholic life.

But that was precisely why the Pope issued it. In various parts of the Church theologians were uttering —not to one another but to the public—views which questioned, or rather denied, almost every element in the doctrine as Catholics had always known it. The Pope must speak or the Eucharist was in peril.

There were theories of Christ's presence in the sacrament which at least sounded like a denial of its reality—the word "real" was preserved but not in any sense of the word "reality" common among men. And the view was spreading that, in whatever sense Christ was present in the sacrament, He was there only to be received as food: so that any other use of the consecrated Host was a superstitious abuse.

Thus in many places visits to the Blessed Sacrament were discouraged—even mocked: the Tabernacle was made almost impossible to find; Benediction was dropped. There were those who added a kind of postscript to all this with an insistence that the Host belonged so totally to one Mass only, that in some places people (seminarians among them) were refusing to receive hosts consecrated at an earlier Mass.

It was in this situation, not universal but existent and spreading, and with more than a beginning of chaos in it, that Pope Paul issued *Mysterium Fidei*.

No Catholic theologian, I have said, denied Christ's presence in the Eucharist: but it is profoundly mysterious, nothing in human experience is in the least like it; the inquiring mind is constantly drawn by it, in a sense tantalized by it, driven to seek for ways of "explaining" it.

Transubstantiation was one such effort, magnificent, rich in itself, rich in suggestion of further depths. But it did not answer every question. Some minds found more satisfaction in it than others. It preserved the essence of the truth Christ had committed to the Church through the Apostles, but it was born of a philosophy not congenial to many of today's thinkers. They felt that there might be another approach to the explication of the mystery.

In *Mysterium Fidei* the Pope does nothing to discourage this. But he insists that the essence of the mystery is inviolate, and he names certain modern theories—"transfiguration", "trans-signification" and others—as not in harmony with it.

What is the essence? Christ had said: "This is my body". The Pope reiterates that the consecrated Host *is* Christ's body, that what the chalice contains *is* his blood. The one looks like bread, the other like wine; they react to every test as bread reacts and wine reacts.

But yet they are not bread, not wine: they cannot be since they are his body, his blood. The Pope quotes St Cyril of Jerusalem: "That which seems to be bread is not bread, though it tastes like it, but the Body of Christ".

"It is presence in the fullest sense", the Pope reminds us, "that is, it is a substantial presence by which Christ, the God-man, is wholly and entirely present". Symbolism will not do as an explanation: after consecration "a new reality is present which may justly be termed ontological, something quite different from what was there before".

This difference, what we may call the "real absence" of bread, is shown as the test. "Presence" is a wide term; there are so many ways of being present.

There is one plain way of being absent, however, namely, not being there. Any solution, the Pope makes clear, must accept the fact that bread and wine are no longer there. The absence of bread is not the most important fact about the Blessed Eucharist, but it is the most instant test of any theory about it.

After the consecration Christ is really, substantially, present: there are the appearances of bread but no bread, of wine but no wine. We are receiving Christ himself within our own being—that is what matters.

Quite *how* this can be we do not know, but for the fact of it we have Christ's word. In comparison with the *fact*, the *how* is of no importance. Yet men long to see deeper, to find explanations—what happens to our Lord's height, for instance, and to his weight? What causes our palates to taste bread as we receive the Host?

Transubstantiation leaves so much still dark. And the Encyclical looks for further exploration of the mystery to arrive at "greater clarity, greater accuracy". But it imposes two conditions: (1) the Reality of Christ's presence must not be dimmed or diminished; (2) no individual may "on his own authority modify the formulas used by the Council of Trent". A theologian may propose modifications or even different theories, discuss them with other theologians, offer them to the Church: but he may not teach them as Catholic doctrine till the Church has approved them. "Unless you shall eat the flesh of the Son of Man and drink His blood you shall not have life in you", says our Lord. With eternal life thus involved, the Eucharist is too important for the faithful to have the speculation of any individual, however richly gifted, imposed upon them.

Obviously every man must read Scripture for himself. But to me it seems that Paul the Saint and Paul the Pope are entirely in accord. "The cup that we bless, is it not the blood of the Lord? The bread that we break, is it not the body of the Lord?" That is in 1 Corinthians 10. In the following chapter come two texts: "He who eats the bread or drinks the cup unworthily will be guilty of profaning the body and blood of the Lord"; "He who eats and drinks without discerning the Lord's body and blood eats and drinks damnation to himself". These would be incredible things to say of any mere symbol, of anything less indeed than what Pope Paul calls "the presence by which Christ the God-man is wholly and entirely present".

But what of the Tabernacle? And visits? And Benediction? What, that is, of the view given wide utterance by theologians but rejected by *Mysterium Fidei*, that the Eucharist was given us by our Lord to be used only as food, given for nourishment *not* for adoration?

As with so very many other problems of either-or, the answer is both. Our Lord did indeed consecrate bread so that it was changed into his Body to be received as food, wine so that it was changed into

his Blood to be received as drink. But he did not say
"only", and common sense not only does not require
"only" but actually excludes it.

It would seem unnatural to the last degree to
concentrate on the nourishing power of the food
while ignoring what the food actually is. Christ our
Lord does not come upon our altars in order to be
adored but to nourish. But he who thus comes *is*
adorable and it would be highly artificial to act as
though we did not know this. Our Lord in the Host
does not become less nourishing by being adored,
and the act of adoration has its own way of nourishing
the human spirit.

There are those who would abolish the Elevation
at Mass on the ground that it was introduced only
because at the time the faithful did not frequently
receive the Eucharist. Maybe so. But how splendidly
the Elevation has justified itself, securing its place in
the Mass on its own merits. Who would wish to forgo
this moment in which we join together in adoring
him whom we are individually to receive?

Christ's body is still present in the Host after Mass,
says the Encyclical. Therefore, although ideally it is
best to receive a host at the Mass of its Consecration,
Hosts consecrated at one Mass may be received at
another and may be received also by the sich where-
ever they may be. These Hosts are normally kept in a
Tabernacle in the Church. The practice grew of
visiting the Church and praying before the Tabernacle in full consciousness of the Presence within it.
Legalistic types extend their objection against the

Elevation even more violently to this practice: they want the Tabernacle to be kept out of sight so that people might not be tempted to adore him who is most certainly there. On the same principle they are against Benediction of the Blessed Sacrament.

Life is larger than logic, especially that kind of logic. The experience of praying before the Tabernacle is its own justification. We rejoiced in the learned defence of it by the Jesuit Karl Rahner. And the Encyclical is wholly for our comfort. "Christ wishes to ensure his presence among us without limits of time"—and his presence calls us to adore. "The faithful should be encouraged to return love for love in visiting the Blessed Sacrament".

You know the jingle:

> Whenever I am near a church
> I go in for a visit
> So that when I am carried in
> Our Lord won't say "Who is it?"

A theologian might blench at that, but as a mere human man he might sometimes find himself repeating it all the same, when no theologians were around —they make one another self-conscious.

III

In all sorts of ways, we feel, Mass is not what is used to be. Let us glance at some of our present discontents.

The discontents are not the same for everybody. I

have mine, you have yours. But there are two main groups of us: those who feel that the changes don't go far enough; and those who loved the Mass as it was.

For the moment we concentrate upon these last. They vary from people, like me, who are unhappy about individual changes, and people to whom any change seems like a rending of some part of their being, a treason against the sacrifice of the Mass itself. It would be wrong to write this off as emotional, irrational. Rationality cannot say everything in religion, any more than in the rest of life; and there are sacred emotions as well as profane or merely neutral.

But, for those who feel like this about the changes, it may be steadying to be reminded that our Roman Mass is the result of a long development. At the Last Supper, our Lord "faced the people" and spoke in Aramaic. If a time-machine could have brought Peter from the first century into ours, he would not easily have followed High Mass in St Peter's—the Latin particularly would have bothered him; he had come to Rome late in life.

Latin is not an eighth sacrament; but those who see something special in it are surely right. It was a newcomer on the Christian scene, but for us of the West it has been prayed in and thought in and taught in as no other language has. There would be an insensitiveness in merely dropping it like a bad habit we have outgrown, and the champions of Mass in Latin have quite an argument in some of the English we are hearing. The translations seem to have been made by scholars who cannot clean from their own pens the Latinity in which they have so long been dipped: much of the phrasing sounds like Latin's vengeance on its supplanter.

The most spectacular oddity is, of course, "Go, the Mass is ended". "Thanks be to God", we reply piously to this incredible statement about a sacrifice which will not "end" while the world endures. Hell must have burst into applause the first time that phrase was heard from the altar. But it is not the only strangeness we hear. I hope it is not disrespectful of me to find myself so often remembering what was once said about something quite different—"The man who wrote that may have ears, for so has another animal. He certainly hasn't an ear".

But we should remember both that our own Church Latin would have sounded monstrous to Cicero, and that the new versions are rush jobs and will be improved. Our real discontents go deeper. I give two of my own, not because I am necessarily right about them but because they enable us to get at what should be the governing principles of change.

I dislike the playing down of the Offertory prayers: the prayer *Deus qui humanae substantiae* contains the sole reminder in the Ordinary of the Mass that we are to be partakers of Christ's divinity: I cannot imagine any hymn valuable enough to drown out that.

I dislike the proposed merging into one, or dropping altogether, of the two Confiteors at the beginning of the Mass. The dropping obviously, but the merging just as certainly, would destroy a dramatic interchange which is a key to the co-operation in worship of priests and lay people. The priest confesses that he has sinned exceedingly, and we pray Almighty God to have mercy on him: then we confess that we are just as bad and the priest prays Almighty God to have mercy on us. Each party has uttered its own unworthiness and accepted the utterance of the others. The Mass can begin.

I may be wrong about either or both of my "dislikes". But a principle is involved. There are those who set up a pattern and by it Liturgy must be measured. It may be what was done in the early Church; or what had been done for centuries; or some Platonic ideal of what a Liturgy ought to be. In none of these patterns are our present human values —our needs, our feelings—allowed for. And without human values Liturgy grows corpse-like. What our Lord said of the Sabbath can be applied here—the Liturgy was made for man, not man for the Liturgy.

Our approach to God *together with others* calls for an accepted order not needed by our private and individual prayers—we cannot all be acting together separately, so to speak. This accepted order is Liturgy. A Liturgy must please God, or its is pointless; but also it must express the mind and heart of the worshippers, or it is lifeless. To keep alive, a Liturgy may have to change.

Rituals which were wholly right for yesterday's man may be empty forms for today's. Rituals developed in one country may be meaningless in another—where we of the West bend the knee, for instance, the Japanese bow; the kissing of the Missal at the Gospel says nothing at all to the Japanese, who are not a kissing people. And within the one country and the one age, there are differences from one man to the next—to one a sanctuary lamp glowing in a dark church is that and no more, to another it can be a reminder that he is not alone in a dark world too powerful for him.

Two principles emerge. The first is that the Liturgy must be formed—and necessary changes in it must be made—not by individuals according to their taste and fancy; not by each pastor for his own congregation, still less by each curate. The Vatican Council has laid it down, in the *Constitution on the Liturgy*, that even a priest may not "add, remove or change anything in the liturgy on his own authority".

The second is that the Liturgy will not accomplish its purpose unless it expresses the mind and heart, the consciousness and even the unconsciousness, of the worshippers. At a given time the authorities might lose contact with the people; but the liturgical expert can be out of contact even more completely.

It is strange, come to think of it, how much time and passion we give to the changes—Latin, dialogue and the like—and how little of either we give to the Mass itself. Yet unless that is alive in us the changes can only galvanize, giving a show of life but no new vitality. A change in the congregation will do more than any number of changes in the Liturgy.

The essence of that profounder change is in the living awareness of what is being done at the altar, and of our active part in it. I have had the chance to hear Catholics questioned on the first point: some thought that our Lord is slain at every Mass; some thought the Mass a meal only with Christ present symbolically; and between these extremes there was devotion but not much clarity.

Remember what Browning says of Mass (in *Easter Eve and Christmas Day*):

> Earth breaks up, time drops away,
> In flows heaven, with its new day
> Of endless life.

That is not to be dismissed as poetry; the phrase "In flows heaven" is precise. Look again at what the two texts we have just discussed (Hebrews 7:24-5, 9:24 and Revelation 5:6 ff.) tell us of the Mass. In Heaven Christ stands always before his Father, presenting himself once slain upon Calvary and for ever living, "interceding" for the salvation of men. At the altar the priest, by Christ's command, in Christ's power, offers that same Christ, present as really, to the same Father for the same purpose. And we take part with the priest in the offering—we and the priest are lifted into one action with the Redeeming Christ.

Did Browning know that? An interesting question. But there is a question that matters more to you an me: Do *we* know it? Upon that we can test ourselves.

Mass and Eucharist

At Mass are we conscious of Christ in heaven "standing as a Lamb slain", "living on to make intercession for us"? Do we remind ourselves of the relation to *that* of what is about to take place at the altar? And of our own part in it, and the part of every other person at Mass with us, and of our consequent oneness with them? Do we even know the three texts? If that is how we do see the Mass, we must see ritual changes as secondary. Latin or Greek or Hottentot, Swahili or Calithumpian, vestments or day-clothes, dialogue or silence, basilica or somebody's house or open sky, altar or kitchen table—how can we spare a thought to these, considering what is actually being done by Christ, by the priest, by ourselves?

Yet the rituals matter. We are not pure spirits, not sheer minds. There is a harmony possible between the spiritual and the material, and liturgy must serve it. We do not join in the offering of the Mass with minds free from care, problems, temptations. Material things—words, gestures, postures—can concentrate us, or leave us unaffected, or add a further distraction of their own. I have seen a quotation from the new Spanish Missal—a man needs "a spiritual counterweight to the whirl of his life". Our Mass *should* be that. May the changes, already made or on the way, help it to be.

Our private prayer is the approach to God of the individual self which each of us uniquely is, and it changes as we change. Liturgy is the corporate approach of men to God (the angels doubtless have

119

their own), and it too will change as men change. It will not change week by week, of course, registering small and perhaps temporary ups and downs of mood.

A Liturgy can, however, come to be seriously out of contact with those who must use it: a period is seen to have ended. That is our position now. Changes have been made. Changes are in the air.

There are Catholics who view with alarm the likelihood of changes yet to be made in Mass and Communion. Mere custom has a way of ringing itself with a kind of sacredness which can pass for the real thing. Thus when the Eucharistic Fast was first reduced to three hours, there were those who still insisted upon fasting from midnight. Yet how much sense there was in the Pacific Islander who, having to walk long miles to Mass, ate a banana on the way and explained his reception of Communion by saying that it was more honourable for his Lord to sit on a banana than for a banana to sit on his Lord. Indeed there seems to be at least as good a case for fasting after Communion as before.

We are less likely to be alarmed at some of the changes we hear proposed if we realize what changes there have already been. I do not mean where the Church has had to forbid wrongful uses of the Sacrament—in the fourth century the Council of Hippo forbade giving the Host to the dead, and the practice persisted for a couple of hundred years after that.

What I have in mind is the changing of practices

not in themselves wrong. As late as 800 years after the Last Supper, it was normal for priests to place the Host in the communicant's right hand, the communicant kissing it and putting it into his own mouth. As late as the fourth century the laity were allowed to take Hosts home with them, receive them privately there, and administer them to others: which is as surprising to us as the visits to the Blessed Sacrament Catholics have been making for the last two centuries would have seemed to them.

Will we perhaps, like the Protestants, have Communion in both kinds—already allowed in a variety of circumstance (at Nuptial and concelebrated Masses, for instance)—for all Catholics at all Masses? Actually it is mere provincialism on our part to think of this as Protestant. Within our own Communion, linked like us to the Pope, nineteen (or is it twenty?) different middle-Eastern and Eastern Churches have it. The early Church had it—it also had the giving of Communion to babies in one kind, the Blood only, in the form of a drop on the tongue. No question of principle is involved.

We hold three facts in mind, two major, one minor. The major are that in receiving under *either* kind, there is nothing of Christ that we do not receive, so that we can receive no more of Him under both; and that the command to receive both was given to the men gathered round Christ at the Last Supper, who were themselves to offer the sacrifice. The minor is that Communion as we receive it, under the appearance of bread, has drawn to it such millions as the

Churches who administer the Chalice have never experienced.

A totally different question is being heard: should Sunday obligation be abolished as the Lenten Fast has been? I am thinking not of Catholics being given the choice of either Saturday or Sunday, but of whether obligation, or any sort of compulsion, has a place here. Most of us, I think, have not given much thought to the question.

But there are those who feel passionately about it. I have heard it urged that one should no more command a man to go to Mass than to get married—love should be the only motive for either. But that is to over-simplify.

Getting married is to be compared not with going to Mass but with becoming a Catholic, and compulsion would indeed be as monstrous in one as in the other. But each condition—being married, being a Catholic—carries with it certain obligations. A man should support his family out of love: but if he doesn't, the law will compel him, physically if necessary.

Out of love for Christ and our fellow-men, we should join with them in offering the Mass. There is no question of physical compulsion; but should the Church make it a grave sin for us not to go to Mass on certain days? It is too complex a question for discussion here. When a particular action is a privilege beyond price—as to join with others in the worship of God certainly is—it may seem like mere legalism to remind ourselves that it may also be a duty.

Ideally we should need no urging, no reminder even, certainly no command. For in the Mass we unite with our Lord in his own worshipping, sacrificing, offering action, and make it ours, make its redeeming powers ours. In the Mass we act as the "royal priesthood" we are, as the co-redeemers we are. Why should we have to be "obliged" to it?

But we must take ourselves as we find ourselves. Realization is our continuing problem. The great spiritual realities do not tug at us, solicit us, build up cravings in our bodily organisms as the world about us does.

For "hunger and thirst after righteousness" does not mean parching in the throat or torment in the entrails. It would be easier for us if it did. We need the Mass, need it urgently, need it more than we need food and drink. But we do not *feel* the urgency in the same way, and plenty of us do not feel it at all.

Many a man is grateful that Sunday Mass is of obligation. Perhaps he cannot imagine staying away. But there were years when the obligation helped to get him there, and there are things the Mass can do to those who take part in it, no matter what brought them to it.

IV

There may be changes that go deeper than any we have glanced at. What we regard as the primary purpose of any institution must affect our attitude to it and all our judgements about it. We are seeing this in the matter of marriage, with procreation no longer holding its solitary pre-eminence. We are seeing the same principle in action, and we may well see it a great deal more, in the matter of the Blessed Eucharist. Christ is really present; therefore he is to be adored.

But Christ is present in this special way in order that he may be received as food. Is adoration primary, or nourishment? We have glanced at this already; we may glance at it again from another angle.

For long the emphasis seemed to be on adoration: hence the infrequent reception—months of preparation regarded as essential—and the fast from midnight. What mattered was the communicant's *fitness* to receive the Adorable One within himself. We are now placing the emphasis where our Lord placed it: on nourishment. What matters most is the communicant's *need*. Where the one consideration used to be to safeguard the honour due to Christ, the whole mind of the Church now is to remove any obstacles in the path of those who need to be fed. Is the food reaching all who need it and could be nourished by it?

How far will this carry us? The question is already being raised about giving the Eucharist to baptized Christians not of our Church. Their need for Christ's Body is not less than ours; their love for him is not less; is their willingness to receive the Sacrament, knowing what we mean by it, condition enough for reception? Permission, we know, has already been given in individual cases.

This matter will press itself on the Church's attention if the offering of Mass in private houses continues and increases—not as a substitute for the parish Mass in Church, but over and above. Might it be possible for the non-Catholic husband or wife who believes our Lord really present to receive him with the rest of the family?

With Mass in private homes, indeed, we seem to have an echo of the Jewish Passover, at which the head of each family presided. Is there likely to be any revival, or development, of this liturgical role for the husband and father? If so there is, as we have seen, a certain hint of a precedent in the early Church.

All these questions are for the Church to decide. But it looks as if we may see a wider admission to Communion than we now know—unbelievers welcomed, perhaps even sinners who are at present barred.

The question is now being seriously asked whether we have been too protective of the dignity of the Sacred Host. Our Lord redeemed the world by submitting his body to publicans and sinners (Luke 7:46), even to those who hated him or slew him. Need the Church be more protective of it in its sacramental presence in which it still works for the redeeming of the world?

We have noted that St Peter might not have found today's High Mass in St Peter's easy to follow. But then, neither would that rather more recent Pope, Pius XII, perhaps.

And changes in the Liturgy—made and still to be

made—are not the only sort. There are those who would be rid of vestments, because our Lord was wearing his street-clothes at the Last Supper. So far, I think, only a minority see anything incongruous in putting colour to use in the usual offering of the Mass; though I seem to notice that in ceremonial wear outside the Sanctuary scarlet and purple cause less excitement than of old. Pageantry is good—while men's hearts are made joyous by it; if they cease to be then it has outlived its usefulness.

Archbishop Mannix, the great Irishman who ruled the Diocese of Melbourne for fifty years, told me of a stranger who came up to him, pointed to his pectoral cross, and said "Christ was not crucified on gold and ivory". The Archbishop remained deep in thought after he had finished telling the story. I was reminded of this incident when at the Council Archbishop Helder Camara urged his fellow bishops to wear crosses made of wood.

In fact a simplification—in vestments, in church buildings, to say nothing of living standards—may be forced on us by something different from a mere change of taste. It may be more like a change of heart. For ourselves to live richly while—in India, say—every day thousands die of starvation is uncomfortable, unless we can manage to switch our minds from it (which we do fairly easily). And to spend upon the glory of God money which might save from starvation all those thousands made in his image does not necessarily give him the glory he wants.

We remember St Ambrose melting down the Church plate to get money to buy back from slavery Roman soldiers captured by the Goths after their victory at Adrianople. The Arians—heretics as it happened—accused him of sacrilege. And he said: "It is far better to preserve souls for our Lord than to preserve gold". When a man was found dead of starvation in a Roman street, Pope Gregory the Great fasted for days. And our own Pope has made clear that the poverty of the world must be a primary concern.